Long-billed curlew, willet, marbled
godwit, Wilson's phalarope, short-billed
dowitchers, Western sandpipers, least
sandpiper, piping plover, snowy plover,
Wilson's plover, semipalmated plover.
Fort Myers, Florida, September.

SHORELINES

BIRDS AT THE WATER'S EDGE

MICHAEL WARREN

Times
BOOKS

Published by TIMES BOOKS,
The New York Times Book Co., Inc.
130 Fifth Avenue, New York, N.Y. 10011

Published simultaneously in Canada by
Fitzhenry & Whiteside, Ltd., Toronto

**Library of Congress Cataloging in
Publication Data**

Warren, Michael, 1938-
    Shorelines: birds at the water's edge.

    1. Shore birds.   I. Title.
QL696.C4W37 1984   598′.33   84-40104
ISBN 0-8129-1133-4

84 85 86 87 88   5 4 3 2 1

Edited and designed by Ian Cameron
Managing editor: Jill Hollis

Produced by Cameron Books,
2a Roman Way, London N7 8XG,
England

Printed in Holland by
drukkerij de Lange/van Leer bv,
Deventer

Frontispiece:
Guillemots and razorbills. Highland
region. June.

Title page:
Great skuas with Arctic skua. Highland
region. June.

Left:
Cedar waxwings. Montauk Point, Long
Island. September.

Right:
Black skimmers and Caspian terns.
Merritt Island, Florida. September.

CONTENTS

PICTURES

Right:
Black-throated divers. Highland region.
June.

Oystercatchers. Islay. January.

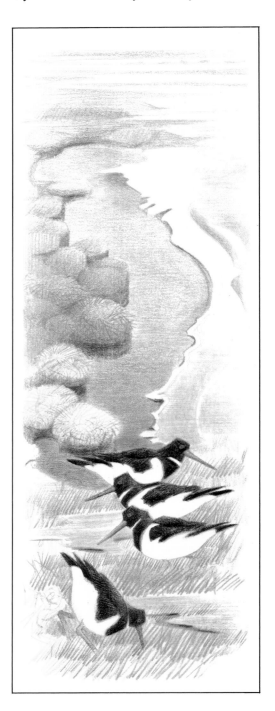

FOREWORD

My bird-watching began along shorelines. The initial spark of enthusiasm first led me to visit reservoirs that were accessible from my home near Wolverhampton in the West Midlands. These were mainly along the A5 road in Staffordshire, at Belvide, Gailey, Chasewater and, later, Blithfield.

From the start, birding has been an aesthetic as well as an ornithological experience for me, with an essentially visual excitement at its core; I spent endless hours around the reservoirs, looking into a magic world, with image after image challenging my early attempts to draw and paint. It was there that the links between birds and water, the theme of this book, became totally imprinted on my mind.

There are other reasons, though, why I have chosen the water's edge as the subject for this book. On the one hand, it provides a huge variety of locations from the gaunt cliffs, sandy beaches and open mudflats of the coast to the banks of rivers, lakes, reservoirs and ponds. Yet a lot that it has to offer is common or at least comparable over a large area: it is the habitat of many of the most wide-ranging species of the northern hemisphere, among them the herring gull, the Sandwich tern and the osprey. Sometimes the same birds will have different names on the two sides of the Atlantic – for example, the American common loon, parasitic jaeger and black-bellied plover are respectively the European great northern diver, Arctic skua and grey plover – and sometimes there are distinct but very similar species such as the American least tern and the European little tern. All this will, I hope, make many of the illustrations evoke images and memories familiar to birdwatchers everywhere from the north of Scotland to the south-eastern United States. There is one final attraction to me in shorelines: as well as being the haunts of water birds and shore birds, they are the best places for seeing migrants – their landfalls after sea crossings. This book is therefore about birds *at* the shorelines rather than birds *of* the shorelines: it has given me the opportunity to paint warblers and waxwings as well as geese and gulls.

Shorelines records two years' birding in Britain, the United States, Holland, France and Portugal during 1982 and 1983. The paintings are the result of particular observations that triggered the desire to make a picture. The stimulus was often a bird's surroundings rather than an intention to paint a particular species. The diary that accompanies the pictures is very far from being an exhaustive account of the birds that I have seen in the two years, but it aims to describe some of the context in which the pictures were painted. Throughout it, I have adopted the convention of using the British name where I have seen a bird in Europe and the American name when I have seen it in the United States.

The paintings are all done with Rowney Flow Formula acrylics on Barcham Green's Pasteless Board, the drawings with Caran d'Ache crayons on Arches paper.

Left:
Brown pelicans with little blue heron and fish crows. Sanibel Island, Florida. September.

Previous spread:
Barnacle geese. Islay. January.

I should like to thank Malcolm Largen and Clem Fisher of Merseyside County Museums, Liverpool, Don Sharp of the Natural History Museum, Wollaton Hall, Nottingham, and the friends who have accompanied me on various trips and helped during the course of my work: Charlie Brown, George Bent II, Martin Davies, Bob Farmer, Roy Galloway, Gordon Ireson, Roger Lovegrove, Tim and Tina O'Sullivan, David Parkin, Alan Richards, Will Russell, David Simon, David Smallshire and Ken Webb.

Michael Warren

Winthorpe,
Nottinghamshire

May 1984

To Kate, Simon and Clara.

Right:
American wigeons and black ducks with ruddy ducks. Jamaica Bay, Long Island, New York. October.

Below:
Ospreys. Merritt Island, Florida. September.

13

BRITAIN: Winter-Spring

ENGLAND

Girton, Nottinghamshire, 2nd January

The worked-out gravel pits at Girton, on the banks of the River Trent, now form a chain of lakes that are used for sailing, and they are a fine place for seeing waterfowl in winter. The heavy snowfalls of December have swollen the normally sluggish Trent enormously; it has reached the top of its flood banks and is still rising. A mile of water faces me as I park my car.

Moving to higher ground, I can see the river pouring through small dykes into the surrounding fields, flooding one area after another with torrents of water. A small group of yellowhammers has found a patch of straw to feed on; they keep eating on their tiny island as the floods sweep around them. Where one would normally expect to see only a few lapwings, there are diving ducks – goosanders and golden-eyes – on open water. As the gravel pits are still frozen except where they have been inundated and there is a layer of water over the ice, the river and the flooded fields have taken their place as the ducks' habitat. Three little grebes are carried on to one of the pits by the flood water.

Girton, 9th January

Today, the sun is shining, there is green grass to be seen, and everything looks tranquil, but it is very cold and there is a lot of snow lying on

Yellowhammers. Girton, Nottinghamshire. January.

Fieldfare. Girton, Nottinghamshire.
January.

the frozen water. Plenty of ducks are flighting around, and in the bend of the river is a good party of wigeon. Eleven dunlins have just landed beside the river. A small party of long-tailed tits flies across it; to them it must seem as wide as the English Channel. Quite a few fieldfares are still around, odd birds that have not gone west with the main flocks and seem to be finding some food here. In these freezing conditions, the water level has dropped at least five feet, leaving great plates of ice in the hawthorn bushes. A pair of pintails is sitting in the shelter of a hedge, the bottom of which is encrusted with large icicles.

As I walk the short distance to Besthorpe, black snow clouds loom up, and the whole area goes grey. Snow starts to whip horizontally across the gravel pits. Among a mass of ducks huddled at one end, only the pinkish-white plumage of the male goosanders peeps out of the general murk. The banks of the gravel pits are rich in seeding

Carrion crows. Girton,
Nottinghamshire. January.

Pintail with wigeons and teal. Girton,
Nottinghamshire. January.

plants, which have attracted a small party of finches. I can just see small, dark shapes moving around. Closer inspection reveals that they are predominantly chaffinches, with redpolls, bullfinches and a brambling among them, but they are very volatile, and my view of them is not very good.

Back at Girton, the only living creatures on the desolate expanse of ice are the black crows which often provide a stark replacement for the myriad ducks when the water freezes. The surrounding landscape is etched with the silhouettes of a few trees. Now the whole area is very quiet. A group of jackdaws flies across. Suddenly there is a call, and a party of fifteen Bewick's swans appears, following the river

17

Goosanders. Girton, Nottinghamshire. January.

down from the north. As soon as they have landed, I go off to look for them and find an almost monochrome scene. The swans are feeding on a small pool in the middle of an icy field, with their heads under the water – fifteen white humps in a grey wilderness. Another few must have joined them, as their number has grown to twenty-one. A solitary lapwing stands on the river bank. Now that the water level has dropped, the Trent has some muddy shoreline on which birds like the lapwing and the dunlins that I saw earlier in the day can forage. At dusk, a small party of goosanders heads up through the cold, grey waters of the river towards the setting sun.

My day ends as the moon rises and I have an idea for a picture: the large winter moon looks rather like an iced peach rising into the grey sky. It makes a fine backdrop to the gull roost on the ice-covered riverside field.

Girton, 10th January

A brilliantly clear day with superb winter light that provides ideal visibility for watching all the ducks. The white sides of the tufted ducks glint on the grey water. Twenty pink-footed geese have just flown south, and the Bewick's swans I saw yesterday have moved up again from grazing on the riverside fields at Besthorpe, a mile to the south – there are twenty-three of them now, as well as a few goosanders. On the edge of the water, amazing frozen structures hang down from the trees. On the grass, frost and partially melted ice form an infinite

18

Duck smews. South Muskham,
Nottinghamshire. January.

variety of patterns, sometimes linking up with the icicles on the larger plants. I have seen a single great crested grebe today – at least they haven't all departed the area. The Bewicks have flown up again and landed at a bend in the river, where I can see them through a tracery of willow branches. On the river banks are snipes in ones and twos. A female sparrowhawk flies lazily but quickly across the pits.

A few miles away, at South Muskham pit in the lee of the A1 road on the outskirts of Newark, to the sound of trains going by, I see another good assortment of ducks. In the middle of them is a great find, though not an unexpected one on a hard January day: three duck smew.

SCOTLAND

Lochgilphead, Argyllshire (Strathclyde), 15th January

A small estuary by the village of Lochgilphead: about fifty greylag geese in a tight group on a sandbar. I sketch them with rocks, seaweed and rock pools in the foreground. The crystal clear sunlight is reflected in the metallic green of the speculums on the wings of teal and wigeon. A jackdaw has landed on a rock in front of the ducks and makes a nice counterpoint with the hooded crows behind them. There are mergansers on the small river that feeds the estuary.

At West Tarbert, where the ferry leaves for Islay, there are small ice floes wedged up into the rocks on the shore of the narrow sea loch, and a lone curlew is picking in the mud among the ice. In the distance are forests and snow-covered hills. A few gulls are wheeling around.

The ferry trip down Loch Tarbert provides the chance to see all three regularly wintering divers, often much closer than is possible from the shore. We see one red-throated diver, two great northerns and sixteen black-throated including a party of nine; apparently, the numbers are more impressive in the early spring. On the loch, and the Sound of Jura into which it opens, are guillemots, black guillemots and razorbills.

Bewick's swans. Girton,
Nottinghamshire. January.

Gull roost. Girton, Nottinghamshire.
January.

Jackdaw, teal, wigeon, hooded crow, greylag geese. Lochgilphead, Argyllshire (Strathclyde). January.

Islay, 16th January

A gloomy, misty morning after listening to the island being lashed by south-westerly gales all night. The main fresh-water loch on Islay, Loch Gorm, is totally frozen, apart from a few puddles of rainwater that have fallen on the ice during the night. I continue on down to search the sand dunes around Machire Bay for choughs, and find about fifteen, at first scattered sightings and then a group feeding on dung. Great rollers are sweeping into the bay from the sea. Although the wind is whipping the sand, it has not entirely obscured what are probably otter tracks. A small pool hidden among the dunes holds teal and wigeon, which have been feeding on its banks. The background here is of fairly sheer sea cliffs. There is a female stone-chat on a rocky wall. I return past Loch Gorm to go towards Loch Gruinart, which cuts deeply into the north side of the island. On the fields, the groups of barnacle geese, some made up of several hundred birds, are tolerant enough of the car to let us have superb views of them, but they do not let us get close enough for my companions to take good photographs. Small boggy patches with tufts of rushes provide a more interesting habitat for the barnacles. In the middle of an area where the rushes are denser, an open space is crammed with barnacles, so densely packed that all the heads seem to come out of a common body. Among the rushes are sallow bushes with twigs that stand out in rich oranges and yellows against the background of dark grey tree masses. A similar habitat holds small groups of whitefronts feeding; others are bathing and preening on a little freshwater pool.

Hen harrier. Islay. January.

At the head of Loch Gruinart, the freshwater Loch Ardnave is virtually frozen, with pools of rainwater lying on the ice and more rain being driven across it by the wind. The only birds are a few oyster-catchers looking rather desolate on the shore, but further round, in the south-east corner of Loch Gruinart, are some superb saltings, still liberally layered with ice and with floes left from the last freeze. On them are good groups of wigeon and barnacle geese. Birds of prey are represented by two sightings each of merlin and hen harrier.

In the evening, barnacle geese come to roost on Loch Indaal. They arrive in small parties to feed on the saltings, gradually forming larger groups and walking out over the tidal mud to their roosting area. As dusk comes, the lights of Bowmore twinkle on the other side of the

Barnacle geese. Islay. January.

Curlew. West Tarbert, Argyllshire
(Strathclyde). January.

Black-bellied plovers. Wellfleet reserve,
Cape Cod, Massachusetts. May.

25

White-fronted geese. Islay. January.

wide loch. The noise of the barnacles yapping increases as more and more fly in, now dropping straight to the roosting area.

Islay, 17th January

The early morning gives us roadside views of barnacle and Greenland white-fronted geese, mainly on fields but also on saltmarshes. This morning, the choughs of Machire Bay can be seen to better advantage, as the sun catches the glossy sheen of their plumage. Today, the male stonechat is there, being pursued by the local cat as it moves along a line of fence posts. In a small rushy valley we find three whooper swans, all adult birds. A buzzard is circling above a nearby wood.

Seen from Port Askaig in the north-east of the island, the sound between Islay and Jura looks very choppy. Out on the white-capped water is a large party of eiders. Jura itself looks forbidding, with low cloud cover and snow patches on the hills.

Just before dusk at Loch Gruinart, the scene is grey, with a shaft of yellow light across the sky picking out reflections in wet mud, still water and tidal rivulets. It makes a fitting background to the roosting barnacle geese.

Glaucous gull and great black-back gull. Islay. January.

Islay, 18th January

A routine stop to look at some goose fields is dramatically enlivened by a peregrine falcon flying quickly through with sharp wings against the strong head wind. It sees three wood pigeons, dives on one in an unsuccessful attempt to kill it, and all the birds vanish in an instant.

At Port Ellen, on the south of the island, I see my first glaucous gull of the winter; it circles and gives a good display. Later, at Bridgend, on Loch Indaal, I see another. On the beach there, a second peregrine swoops in low over some trees and nearly takes a redshank at the water's edge. The loch itself is quite productive today. Sea-watching there produces a flock of over a hundred scaup, looking splendidly austere in colour, and a Slavonian grebe, just coming into breeding plumage. Two purple sandpipers cling to a small sea-washed rock covered in seaweed.

On the return ferry to West Tarbert, the count of divers is better than it was three days ago: five red-throated, seven great northern and eleven black-throated.

Red-necked grebe. Sutton-on-Sea,
Lincolnshire. February.

Smew and goldeneye. Girton. March.

Besthorpe, Nottinghamshire, 6th February

The worked-out gravel pits here have not been kept for recreational purposes like the ones at Girton; some of them have been filled in with fly ash from the Electricity Board's power stations and are given over to winter wheat. There is still an active washing system for gravel, and this has resulted in some of the ground becoming marshy. In the three weeks since I was last here, the whole scene has changed: the flood waters have gone, and the bird population is back to normal.

I arrive to find a hunt on its way through the gravel pit area – about fifty riders looking incongruous in their scarlet and black coats as they plod along the muddy banks with their hounds. They soon disappear, taking their followers with them, and the birds do not seem to have been at all disturbed by them.

I can see over two hundred wigeons, a splendid pair of pintails, goosanders, teal, and thirteen shelducks, which look very bright in the sunlight. At least one jack snipe has managed to survive the hard spell. Some 120 golden plover come sidling in through the sunlight, bronze where their wings catch the sun but black against the sky. On the tail of the party as they fly past are six dunlins. Later, I find them all again on a wheat field that is still partly flooded. With them are a few redshanks and an assemblage of gulls, mostly black-headed with a few great black-backs. Some herons are standing at the back on the edge of a dyke.

Lincolnshire, 21st February

On a day trip, I see a splendid red-necked grebe on a small roadside pit near Sutton-on-Sea, north of Skegness. The nearby Anderby area provides typical beach sightings: Brent geese, scoters, snow buntings and a few waders – bar-tailed godwits, sanderlings and turnstones.

Besthorpe, 27th February

There have been distinct changes in the duck population here over the past fortnight or so. Most of the mallards and several of the goosanders are now paired, and the wigeon have gone, greatly reducing the overall number of waterfowl. On the winter wheat fields, which still carry some surface water, there are waders: about twenty dunlins, with lapwings and a few redshanks, plus about 150 golden plovers on drier ground behind. Further along the river bank, there are two ruffs among about fifty starlings.

In a marshy area, some blue tits fly past me into the reedmace. They are very active, climbing up and down the stems to feed on the heads, pulling out tufts of seeds, some of which float away. Quickly, they have gone again.

In another part of the marsh is a pool-side hawthorn bush that I discovered a fortnight ago held a roost of corn buntings. Last time, I could hardly see more than their silhouettes, but today, coming earlier, I can see them in the light. I have seen eighteen so far, but I shall stay to watch them for a while...

Girton, 20th March

The water is almost clear of bird life, except on a small pool, where there is a quiet group of goosanders preening. A small influx brings mainly tufted ducks and, darting around right in the centre of them, a single male smew. He puts on a courtship display for the benefit of a female goldeneye: he draws his head right back, seeming to push his body back into the water, then springs up vertically, bobs back and twists from side to side. What a superb bird – it is curious how many of the finest birds have black and white plumage.

Besthorpe, 27th March

A warm, very still, grey day on the edge of spring. All the birds seem to be paired: mute swans, great crested grebes, mallards and sixteen shelducks. A lot of wigeons, 110 in all, and eleven goldeneyes are getting ready to move north. A few of the winter waders, dunlins and redshanks, are still around. The redshanks' song is beginning to trip through the air, and there are lapwings crying – definite signs of spring. Another week should bring the migrants in. Among about seventy golden plovers on a field of winter wheat are quite a few northern birds which are assuming their breeding dress of black, white and gold. The flock runs hither and thither, always cautious and watchful.

Besthorpe, 4th April

The first spring migrants have arrived, and the day is sunny, with soft southerly winds. The call of the little ringed plover echoes around the gravel pits; a single bird is calling continuously, no doubt hoping to attract others of its species. Two sand martins are flicking over the small pool where one of the pair of mute swans is sitting on its nest. With any luck, the nest will escape vandalism this year. Seven red-shanks and seven ruffs are feeding on an area of mud. Only three of the goosanders remain now, and a single goldeneye. The shelduck are down to fourteen, mostly paired, although they are still display-ing, with their heads down, first retracted and then forced forward, running towards and then past each other on the mud, while the rest of the group watch interestedly and wait their turn.

Besthorpe, 10th April

Cool northerly winds now after the warmth of last weekend. The two sand martins have gone, and no swallows have appeared yet. The num-ber of goosanders has gone up to seventeen, including three drakes, and the shelduck are at sixteen, but not displaying. Perhaps they have been discouraged because the area they were running around on at the weekend is flooded again. There are two ringed plovers on the winter wheat and now a pair of little ringed plovers doing their display flight around the pits. Only twenty-one golden plovers remain, but there is a good selection of waders: a fine oystercatcher and, sitting among fourteen ruffs, a spotted redshank calling continuously while it is on the ground. It still has most of its grey winter plumage, but the dark summer feathers are beginning to come through, particularly on the belly, which has clear black barring. Two fresh-as-paint male wheatears are another sign that the migrants are coming in, and so are two yellow wagtails looking brilliantly coloured in the sunlight.

WALES

Elan Valley, near Rhayader, Powys, 11th-13th April

The large reservoirs of the Elan Valley are surrounded by forests, moorland hills and crags. Immaculate goosanders can be seen flighting against the hills and the dark water. Among eleven goldeneye are two displaying drakes. But the valley is less notable at the moment for waterfowl than for raptors: kestrels, buzzards, sparrowhawks and, most excitingly, kites, which drift above moor and woodland, coming down to fly near the edge of the lake, then away again to circle and

Red Kite. Elan Valley, Powys. April.

bank against their chosen wood. I have a superb view of a peregrine falcon as it careers in over a rocky ridge and flashes across the rock face to land high above the lakeside.

ENGLAND

Besthorpe, 17th April

Three pairs of redshanks and two of great crested grebes have now settled in. Around the marsh, there are shoveler ducks courting. I can count ten ruffs, and a lone sand martin represents the small migrants.

Besthorpe, 24th April

The number of ruffs feeding on the fields has increased to fifteeen, and there are more yellow wagtails now, including a pale primrose bird which is away before I can study it.

South Muskham, Nottinghamshire, 1st May

North-westerly winds are raging across the pits, lashing the water into waves, and the swallows look more like petrels in an October gale than birds seeking food on a May lake.

Besthorpe, 9th May

A complete transformation from last weekend, but there is a lot of mud left by the storms. On it, I see my first good bird of the day, a greenshank, which is keeping company with the resident redshanks. There are brimstone and orange-tip butterflies fluttering around the hedgerows. Sedge warblers and whitethroats are singing – they have all come in this weekend. With the woodland birds that I saw earlier today – nightingale, redstart, turtle dove, garden warbler – there are all the signs of the last few days having seen a big influx.

Peregrine falcon. Elan Valley, Powys. April.

Snowy egrets with osprey. Rocky Neck
State Park, Connecticut. May.

UNITED STATES: Spring

Great Island, near Old Lyme, Connecticut, 17th May

My first American location is a flat, brackish marsh on the Connecticut coast, very bare and open, with only grasses, bulrushes and the like for cover. Out on the marsh, stands have been built for ospreys to nest on. Several of the nests are occupied – I can see two with pairs of birds, and there is another with a sitting bird. One osprey is eating a fish, tearing at it with his beak. Ospreys are so rare in Britain that it is extraordinary to see them here in such numbers.

On the water of one of the tidal channels that run through the marsh are some least terns, which are calling excitedly. Three glossy ibises fly over the marsh and drop out of sight. One or two crows and larger gulls are drifting around and can be mistaken momentarily for ospreys.

On the far side of the island, an old lighthouse tower gives some sense of scale to the expanse of marsh. Away across the channel is a glistening sandbar. A cormorant is moving slowly down the channel, and a green heron flies low over the reeds, drops down into them and then comes back into sight. Red-winged blackbirds are everywhere, and grackles come and go among the marsh vegetation. Some nearby bushes hold a song sparrow and a yellow warbler. It is the ospreys, though, that hold pride of place today.

Earlier, as we crossed the old Black Hall River bridge, we thought we saw an egret diving down. On the way back, we find a snowy egret on the river bank, and down in the water are several waders. They are lesser yellowlegs, with spangled plumage on their backs and ochre legs, which are visible as they probe in the mud below the water for food. In another creek, empty now that the tide is out, there is a whole pack of birds. They seem all to be black-bellied plovers, but my view is rather distant and the wet mud of the basin is shimmering and glinting in the sunlit haze.

Rocky Neck State Park, Connecticut, 17th May

We drive down to the beach through woods interspersed with marshy areas, little rivers and tidal creeks. Another osprey nest on a man-made wooden stand is much closer than the others and provides a fine view of the head of the sitting bird. Its mate comes to the nest, and the two birds fill the field of the telescope lens. Some snowy egrets are feeding in a creek, which also has some waders: a killdeer flies away, showing its orange tail, and there are more lesser yellowlegs. A few tiny waders in the far distance are not identifiable through the haze.

Trumbull, Connecticut, 18th May

A very suburban shoreline: at the bottom of my host's garden, just as it turns into woodland, is a little marshy hollow through which the water moves sluggishly. Around it are broad-leaved plants, rushes and a thicket of sallows, which contain a swamp sparrow, a perky little bird with a bright red, rusty cap, and a yellowthroat, a smart-looking warbler with a black facial patch and yellow below its bill. Both seem rather shy – you get a fairly good glimpse of them now and again, but generally they remain hidden.

Rocky Neck State Park, 19th May

On the edge of a marsh, there are snowy egrets and green herons to sketch as well as large numbers of diminutive waders, most of which

Yellowthroat and swamp sparrow. Trumbull, Connecticut. May.

Green heron with red-winged blackbird. Rocky Neck State Park, Connecticut. May.

33

seem to be least sandpipers. They have greenish-ochreous legs and go around with darting movements as they feed. Suddenly, everything is looking up and getting up: herons' necks stretch into the air, heads turn and the waders fly off, calling as they go. I look up, and there, coming in over the trees, is a marsh hawk. It is a rather dilapidated specimen with several of its secondary feathers missing. The marsh hawk (which is more correctly known as the northern harrier) is the American equivalent of the European hen harrier. It glides around above the marsh and then flies lazily away over the far wood.

Cape Cod, Massachusetts, 21st May

Wellfleet is a sanctuary owned by the Massachusetts Audubon Society. The first thing I observe is a nice juxtaposition of very different species: the bright blue iridescence of a grackle and, bobbing alongside, a spotted sandpiper. On another pool are green herons, lesser yellowlegs, and a solitary sandpiper; red-winged blackbirds are singing, and swallows are flying around. Further out, a lot of black-bellied plovers (the same species as the European grey plover) make a striking sight in their black and silver plumage against the green marsh grass. Also out there are more lesser yellowlegs, a semipalmated plover and one or two 'peeps' – the general name for the smallest American sandpipers – but at this range I cannot identify the species. On another small pool is a greater yellowlegs and a group of the tiny waders flying around. This time, they are close enough to identify as semipalmated sandpipers, and there is a semipalmated plover with them.

On the sand dunes, there are low bushes with sparrows singing in them, and two eastern kingbirds, larger relations of the flycatchers, with black heads, grey backs and white-edged tails. A horned lark flies across the path and lands on a small patch of sand – this is the same species as the European shore lark, but rather different in the reddish, sandy colour on the back of the neck. Eleven red-breasted mergansers form a line offshore, and I can see a black duck down in the marsh. A sandy spit holds a typical gathering of great black-back gulls, and a sprinkling of tiny waders feeds nearby as another flight of about five yellowlegs comes in.

Green heron. Rocky Neck State Park, Connecticut. May.

Spotted sandpiper and grackle. Wellfleet reserve, Cape Cod, Massachusetts. May.

At least thirty black-bellied plovers are on an area of marsh grass as the tide creeps in and moves the birds about; they call as they go. Their plumage ranges from the absolute black and white of the full breeding dress through blackish brown to birds that are immature or just coming out of their winter plumage, which are paler and flecked with dark brown and touches of black.

The bay is edged with rocky humps covered with pines. Out towards the glistening sandbars, there are about twelve mergansers and with them a couple of black ducks. Further out on the sand are a pair of laughing gulls in their black-hooded summer dress. The swallows that are darting everywhere are barn swallows, much richer in colour underneath than the European swallow. In the distance, over the bay, is a cloud of waders – the wheeling flocks look like smoke blown by the wind as they are moved on by the advancing tide.

On one of the small rocky outcrops, the woodland is full of warblers. I see myrtle, chestnut-sided, magnolia, black-and-white, Canada and Wilson's warblers. The jewel-like quality of these American warblers is a stunning change from the mainly subdued colours of their European equivalents.

The Atlantic side of the Cape Cod coast was the landing point of Marconi's first transatlantic telegraph cable. By the Marconi station is a white cedar swamp, which appears to be quite birdless apart from a single great crested flycatcher. Tomorrow, I will try it again earlier in the morning.

Coming down to the beach, we find ourselves on a sand cliff, a great ribbon that runs in both directions to beyond the horizon. The blue sea with its white-topped breakers is covered in the most incredible array of ducks, a great raft of birds that must stretch for at least a mile and a half. The vast majority of them must be white-winged scoters – all those I have seen flying have white wing patches. There are a few mergansers among them, and possibly the odd scaup, but they are a long way out and specific identification is difficult.

Cape Cod, 22nd May

My early morning visit to the white cedar swamp by the Marconi station does not produce much. A black-capped chickadee is working its way through the swamp. A pair of blue jays flutters out of the trees; they glint and flash in the shafts of sunlight as they tumble downwards. The great crested flycatcher is still around and rufous-sided towhees are kicking vigorously at the leaves on the ground. I can hear the strident call of a resident species of woodpecker, the flicker, but, disappointingly, there are no warblers.

We drive through Provincetown to reach the tip of the Cape Cod peninsula, a final sandy finger rather similar to Blakeney Point in Norfolk. On a pebbly section of beach, a pair of least terns obligingly land in front of me, obviously prospecting for a nesting site. The tide is right up at the moment; on the inner marshes, bunches of black-bellied plovers and other waders are flighting. A common loon, which in Britain we would call a great northern diver, flies through, resplendent in its breeding plumage, with black head and white collar. A pair of Sandwich terns career wildly overhead, kirricking madly.

At the end of this particular sandspit, a channel of water separates me from its main continuation. On the end is a massive gathering of gulls. There are also some more least terns and about forty common terns, many more of which are fishing in the bay. Another mass of gulls includes great black-backs, herring, ring-billed and one or two laughing gulls. On our way back out of Provincetown, we pause near Pilgrim Lake and watch red-winged blackbirds on the marsh.

Black-capped chickadee. Marconi Station, Cape Cod, Massachusetts. May.

Least terns. Provincetown, Massachusetts. May.

In the afternoon, we return to the Wellfleet Audubon reserve to search in vain for piping plovers on their usual beach. The tide has receded now, and there are a lot of black ducks standing out on the bay with large numbers of black-bellied plovers. A greater yellowlegs and some smaller waders fly over. I find a horseshoe crab stranded in the mud and observe another swimming down the channel – weird, prehistoric-seeming creatures.

Again at Wellfleet in the evening, there are a solitary sandpiper and a greater yellowlegs on the marsh, and a female black duck working her way across the marsh with eight or nine ducklings, little yellow and brown creatures dotting in and out of the weed with their mother moving solicitously among them. Just as I put my bird-watching gear away for the day, a marsh hawk glides in close over the parking lot and disturbs some grackles, which flee.

Cape Cod, 23rd May

On the beach by the old Coastguard station near Nauset, a large tidal inlet separates off a long spit of sand running parallel to the line of the coast. The sand is scored with strange patterns made by horseshoe crabs, probably in the night: circles with diagonal thrusts across them.

I have come looking for piping plovers and immediately find two pairs and a nest with four eggs. The birds scurry away with quicksilver speed across the sand. Twenty to thirty pairs of least terns are breeding on this ideal flat expanse of sand. In Britain, it would be fenced off and protected, but here it is open to the public. A mass of waders is

Red-winged blackbird. Pilgrim Lake,
Massachusetts. May.

gathering on the tidal flats. The majority are dunlins, each with a
black belly and a smart rusty red back. Among them are a few yellowlegs, which I think are greater yellowlegs, and further out a few
peeps, too far away to identify.

Black duck and ducklings. Wellfleet
reserve, Cape Cod, Massachusetts. May.

Piping plovers. Nauset, Massachusetts. May.

Mount Desert Island, Maine, 24th May

The forests of the Acadia National Park run from the mountains down to the coast. The rocky shoreline with crashing waves is interrupted by bays, inlets and rivers. The first bird we see is a belted kingfisher at the roadside; it sits facing out where a small river enters the harbour and nearly produces a traffic accident.

In the forest are black-and-white warblers, Canada warblers and golden-crowned kinglets. On the coast are eider ducks, red-breasted mergansers and black guillemots. A purple sandpiper perches on a wave-washed rock. It is all reminiscent of Scotland, but on a rather larger scale. The difference is that you can turn from watching the species that are very familiar in Scotland and suddenly be confronted by brilliantly coloured American wood warblers in the trees.

We have come to a bay with two small, low islands of the local rock, which shades from grey through to orangey pink. One of them has a lot of double-crested cormorants standing on it, while the other has herring, great black-back and laughing gulls. Some more black guillemots are swimming offshore. Another thing that Maine has in common with Scotland is that it is also cold and wet.

A smaller, pebbly cove with quite a bit of seaweed has five spotted sandpipers. Some of them are disturbed by another lot of humans and fly across the small creek to land on a great expanse of rock that slopes down steeply into the water, where they run about teetering anxiously. The place is curiously reminiscent of little bays in the Scilly Isles, off the tip of Cornwall, where the spotted sandpiper turns up as an autumn

Belted kingfisher. Mount Desert Island, Maine. May.

Spotted redshanks with curlew
sandpipers, little stints, dunlins, ruffs,
avocets, curlews, black-tailed godwits,
knot, bar-tailed godwit. North Norfolk.
August.

vagrant. Quite a number of small birds are active on the seaweed. At least two or three myrtle (or, more correctly, yellow-rumped) warblers are feeding on it among the pebbles, as well as a small brown stripey bird that proves to be a song sparrow. Another warbler, a male northern parula with a beautiful blue head, and yellow and chestnut on its breast, lands in the pines above us. The trees are not very tall, and

Purple sandpiper. Mount Desert Island, Maine. May.

Spotted sandpipers. Mount Desert Island, Maine. May.

Myrtle warblers and song sparrow.
Mount Desert Island, Maine. May.

walking through them, I am reminded of the pine forests around the Mediterranean, just as I was by the extensive pine forests around Cape Cod, where the trees are also rather low, although they do not have the scent of the Mediterranean pines.

I can now see that there are three myrtle warblers on the seaweed and stones, one female and two males, which are richer in appearance than the female, with black, yellow, blue and grey plumage.

Mount Desert Island, 25th May

This morning, I start by looking at the freshwater area of the island, a small river and the adjacent marsh. Not a lot of birds are to be seen apart from the tree swallows that are flitting around and are easily distinguishable by the contrast between the sharp blue-green of their backs and their white underparts. A few barn swallows mingle with them. One or two sparrows are singing among the grasses of the marsh. A great blue heron passes overhead on his way to his daily feed.

Moving down to the shore area, I disturb a pair of spotted sandpipers, which must be on their breeding territory. They fly out to the rocks, from which they watch me. An eastern kingbird is perching on a log on the shore, and today there are a lot of warblers: yellow, myrtle and black-throated green warblers. In the trees on the edge of this piece of rocky coast, which is curiously named Wonderland Beach, there are even more warblers – northern parula, magnolia, Blackburnian and again myrtle and black-throated green – as well as a slate-coloured junco.

Jamaica Bay, New York, 28th May

Jamaica Bay is part of the National Gateway Park which is just outside New York, close to Kennedy Airport. It is an excellent place for birds, particularly migrants: a large expanse of saltmarsh with lagoons and of marshland with freshwater pools, reedbeds and bushy areas. The first birds I see are a few double-crested cormorants and about thirty brants (or, as they are called in Britain, Brent geese) lingering on from the winter. One of the black ducks I can see has a brood, which must have hatched at about the same time as the ducklings I saw at Wellfleet. There are other ducks as well: gadwalls and northern shovelers (both species that also appear on the eastern side of the Atlantic as well), and a large party of ruddy ducks. These are very striking birds, particularly the males, which have handsome chestnut plumage, black and white heads and bright blue bills. They are commonly established now in the West Midlands in England, but it is nice to see them in their native North America. In flight, there are a few red-breasted mergansers, ring-billed and laughing gulls, least and common terns, and what for me is the biggest excitement of the day, a black skimmer. This is built like a rather racy gull, black above, white below, and with an enormous carrot-like bill, which has a short upper mandible and a long lower one, both of them red at the base and black at the tip. As its name implies, the black skimmer flies low with its lower mandible actually trailing in the water to collect its food. After a while, this one settles on a sandy bank with a brant and a pair of shovelers, a rather incongruous collection of species.

I can see a number of snowy egrets, some close, some far away on the marsh, and also great egrets, which, apart from their different size, are recognisable by having a yellow bill, black legs and black feet, where the snowies have a black bill, black legs and yellow feet. It would be interesting to know how this difference in the distribution of colours evolved. There is another member of the heron family flying across, a slightly dumpy grey bird which proves to be a black-crowned night heron. There are also green herons on the marshes.

One of the birds you can expect to see on the coastal marshes of the north-eastern seaboard is the glossy ibis, which I associate in Europe with the southern Mediterranean marshes of Spain and, further east, with Greece. Here they are quite well established and are spreading. We have several good sightings of ibises flying by and feeding in the marsh grass. There is an American oystercatcher, brownish on its back where the European bird is solidly black.

As on the marshes on Cape Cod and up in Maine, there is no shortage of black-bellied plovers; one group must number about seventy birds. Sprinkled among them are turnstones, short-billed dowitchers and dunlins. Turnstones, which are called ruddy turnstones in North America, have very striking plumage: their backs are red with black markings and elsewhere they are black and white. There are also semipalmated plovers and a single killdeer walking through the grass. Most of the seven short-billed dowitchers are in their rich summer plumage. The dunlins here are much brighter than European ones. The North American birds used to be called red-backed dunlin, and indeed their backs are definitely more of an orangey-red colour; their appearance is generally cleaner, with whiter white and blacker black, altogether laundered-looking. Although there are many parties of semipalmated sandpipers, we search in vain for least sandpipers.

Black skimmers, brant, northern shoveler, red-winged blackbird, glossy ibis, ruddy turnstone. Jamaica Bay, New York. May.

BRITAIN: Summer–Autumn

ENGLAND

Besthorpe, 6th June

The summer heat is now bearing down on the flat plain of the Trent Valley, which has the hard, dry look of midsummer. A small colony of black-headed gulls is nesting in the rushes – isolated clumps out in the water make good sites, and several bulky nests have already been completed. The birds are flying noisily overhead. Some of them share the fence posts out in the water with a lone common tern, while others balance on a pile of gravel. Occasional snatches of sedge warbler song come from the waterside vegetation. A few sand martins are flying back and forth across the surface of the water. There are four non-breeding mute swans as well as the resident pair, which are cruising around with four youngsters trailing behind them – it is good to see that they have managed to raise a brood of cygnets this year. Among the ducks – largely mallards preparing to moult – are a few shovelers, which I would expect, and a drake wigeon, which is a surprise.

Further along the bank, where it is much marshier, there is a party of about thirty lapwings – their starting to gather is a sure sign of midsummer. Beyond the main group of mallards and shovelers are a few smaller ducks, and among them I spot a pair of garganeys – my first record of a pair here. My only previous sighting of a garganey in the Trent Valley was of a single bird one November, but I have long hoped to see spring birds here, as the habitat is perfect for them to nest in. I have moved round now, and the garganeys have returned to the pool and settled. Through the telescope, I get good views of the drake with his flash of white eye-stripe.

The sparse vegetation on a dry, sun-baked bed of fly ash holds a pair of vociferous ringed plovers – no doubt they have young hidden away among the plants and are wanting me to go away. A group of five herons lifts lethargically, flies ploddingly away and disappears to a new resting place. I have moved round to a better position, with the sun behind me so that I have a much closer view of the garganeys. The drake wigeon is there, too. The amount of activity among the redshanks shows that they have also got young hidden away. An unusual sight: three cuckoos together, flying towards Besthorpe village.

Besthorpe, 8th June

Late evening: I arrive just before eight o'clock. It is rather overcast after another hot day. I was hoping to see the garganeys again, but there is no sign of them, although most of the other ducks are still here and have been joined by a gadwall. Two redshanks occupying perching posts are chip-chip-chipping incessantly against a background of general hubbub, with the black-headed gulls putting in their usual contribution. A green sandpiper flies through – a nice surprise. I'm not sure if I actually disturbed him, but he was well in flight when I first saw him, making his way south. When you see these birds in June, you don't know if they are heading north or south, or just hanging around. Another background noise of summer is the turtle dove calling and singing. The shelducks have had some success in breeding, but not much – I can see ten adult birds with two ducklings trailing along behind them, although perhaps there are more secreted somewhere. Today's other surprise is a pair of curlews in the hay field.

Garganeys. Besthorpe, Nottinghamshire. June.

Besthorpe, 12th June

On a cooler, showery day, I am again on the quest for garganey. I even work the small marsh to see if they have moved in there for breeding, but there is no sign of them. They must have departed. Instead, I get a bonus: a pair of ruddy shelducks – fine birds, quite elegant in flight, with striking orange-brown plumage, pale heads and black and white wings. Usually classed as escapes in Britain, they could very possibly be genuine vagrants. They are obviously quite happy to have found this shallow lake with a sandy bottom and shore, which may well be reminiscent of their proper home, possibly in the south of Spain or in eastern Europe, around the Caspian Sea, or even in North Africa.

Besthorpe, 3rd July

Things are better here than when I came earlier in the·week on an evening visit that happened to coincide with some illegal shooting. I saw one mallard downed, and a distinct lack of birds, particularly of ducks, revealed that there had been some earlier unpleasantness. Today, I can see a female tufted duck with five ducklings, signifying another breeding success, and there is more wader activity. The ringed plovers have also managed to raise two young, which are at the moment resting at the edge of the water on a flat piece of reclaimed land that also contains quite a good gathering of lapwings, standing out blackish green against the lumps of bare earth. A large sandy pool has been drained only for the past three or four days, and the waders are already there: three dunlins, a greenshank, two green sandpipers and a ruff – a good start to the return wader migration.

Besthorpe, 17th July

Basking under a hot sun are a few ducks in eclipse plumage – shoveler, teal, tufted – and a party of about seven Canada geese, probably a family group and also in eclipse. The family of swans, still with four cygnets, is lazing on a well-flattened hummock of grass and sedge. There must be about two hundred lapwings now in the flock, and the numbers of little ringed plovers and snipes are increasing, as birds, fresh from their breeding grounds, start to gather for the autumn.

   A pair of reed warblers starts scolding from some of the herbage on the bank. I have not recorded them here before this year, and I am not sure whether they have just deserted another breeding ground or whether they have been here for some time and I have missed them. As both birds scold away, they are joined by a sedge warbler.

Flamborough Head and Bempton Cliffs, Humberside, 23rd July

My first ever visit to a famed ornithological hot-spot. The head is quite impressive with its limestone cliffs, and the beach is very contrasty with mainly blackish brown, but also red and green, seaweed against the white and occasional grey of the limestone pebbles and rocks. One cove with a stack rising out of it has rock pipits and pied wagtails on the beach and house martins flitting around – I will probably make it into a picture. Looking out to sea from the cove, I can see a constant stream of sea birds: kittiwakes, fulmars, shags, gannets, guillemots, razorbills, puffins, Sandwich terns.

   The nearby Bempton Cliffs have points where you can get very close views of kittiwakes on the nest and of puffins, looking as quizzical as ever. From the hedges of the cliff-top fields, the metallic trill of the corn buntings seems very musical in comparison with the cries of the sea birds. Increasing numbers of gannets are to be seen as I approach their breeding spot, the only mainland colony in Britain. Some of the

Juvenile ringed plovers. Besthorpe, Nottinghamshire. June.

Mute swans and cygnets. Besthorpe, Nottinghamshire. July.

young are very large, white and downy like expensive cuddly toys. On a still, sunny July day, it would be great just to stand here watching them. As it is, a brisk north-easter is blowing constant drizzle, with gusts of rain. The paramount sensation, though, in great sea bird colonies is of noise – something you cannot convey in paintings.

Flamborough Head, 24th July

On an early morning sea-watch, I can mainly see the resident birds moving up and down the coast. However, I manage to find four or five Manx shearwaters out at sea, and a lone great skua ploughing his way against the wind.

Besthorpe, 1st August

The month has begun wet, warm and very misty. As the water level is up, there is not much wader activity. Seven heron shapes disappear off into the gloom. Some common terns – three adults and a juvenile – are squabbling overhead. The family of swans is still making progress. Sedge warblers are carrying food; there are many young ones around. A lone little ringed plover calls out of the mist. Tagging along at the end of a small party of mallards flushed from one of the pools is a garganey, the first I have recorded since the pair I hoped would breed at the beginning of June, and probably unrelated.

Besthorpe, 8th August

A pleasant, sunny morning, and the water level leaves lots of exposed mud, which has brought the waders back: three greenshanks, one or two common sandpipers, a green sandpiper, a little ringed plover and a ruff. A piping sound heralds the arrival of a trio of oystercatchers. There are herons and snipes in plenty, and moorhens with their young. The number of mallards has now risen to about a hundred, with a smaller number of teal and shoveler among them. Many turtle doves, and a few feral pigeons, are drinking and resting.

Gannets, kittiwakes, puffins. Bempton Cliffs, Humberside. July.

Right:
Pied wagtail with house martins. Flamborough Head, Humberside. July.

51

Near Anderby, Lincolnshire, 15th August

A day on the beach is enlivened by watching the ringed plovers evading holidaymakers and dogs.

Ringed plover. Anderby, Lincolnshire. August.

North Norfolk, 26th August

The Titchwell reserve of the Royal Society for the Protection of Birds, among the salt marshes and sand dunes of the North Norfolk coast, is alive with birds and has a fine late summer assembly of waders. Twelve feet away from one of the hides is a superb spotted redshank in an elegantly cross-legged pose which I will endeavour to sketch. The other waders I can see are curlew sandpipers, little stints, wood sandpipers, greenshanks and multitudes of dunlins and ringed plovers. In addition, there are coots, ducks, cormorants, herons and Canada geese. I can see bearded tits among the reeds, and a marsh harrier is flying over the reedbeds. Most exciting of all, there are four spoonbills on the other side of the lagoon, sleeping most of the time and rarely showing off their amazing bills.

Down on the shore, a few sanderlings just beginning to lose their summer plumage are running around on the tideline. Among various terns, there is a pair of little terns. These nest at Titchwell, but are usually gone by this time of year – it is a stroke of luck to find a pair still here. In the tidal creek at the back of the shingle where the terns breed are a lot of waders: knots, dunlins, oystercatchers, turnstones and about thirty bar-tailed godwits, all pushed in by the high tide. In flight, the godwits are sharp and black against the sky – you start to notice the rich buffs and rusts when they come down against the land. A single grey plover still sports its magnificent summer plumage.

Twenty miles to the east at Cley-next-the-Sea, a Norfolk Naturalists' reserve of saltmarshes and reedbeds interrupted by muddy channels, there is a good sprinkling of waders, mainly the species I have seen at Titchwell. A vociferous party of Sandwich terns keeps taking flight, wheeling and tumbling. Seven whimbrels fly over with a single bar-tailed godwit. Bearded tits are calling from the reedbeds.

As I walk up on to the shingle bank that separates the marshes from the sea, two black terns beat their way along the shoreline, flicking dark as they dive into the water. Quite a few common and Sandwich terns are also moving west. Avocets are feeding and standing in the North Hide Pool, which is full of eclipse ducks. I finally arrive at the tiny Eye Pool just ahead of a thunderstorm. As I am settling down to sketch two curlew sandpipers and two little stints that are really close, the heavens open and I race for the car. The storm is quite fierce and lasts for an hour or so. When it clears, I follow up the one piece of hard news I have picked up since arriving and go to Salthouse, two miles further east, to look for a Baird's sandpiper, a rare vagrant from North America. When I get there, I am greeted by the usual tale: it was certainly there right up to the start of the thunderstorm.

Cley, 27th August

A pre-breakfast excursion to Salthouse to look for the Baird's sandpiper is a failure, so I buy a permit for the hides at Cley marshes, where I find a seething mass of birds. A squadron of black-tailed godwits, about thirty of them, flies in and settles among the other waders, which are curlews, a few whimbrels, bar-tailed godwits, many ruffs, curlew sandpipers and dunlins. There are plenty of ducks, all uniform in their drabness – I can never raise the enthusiasm really to look at ducks in August when they are all in eclipse. I return to the Eye Pool and make the sketches of the curlew sandpipers and little stints that the thunderstorm interrupted yesterday.

Then news comes through that the Baird's sandpiper may be back on its favourite pool – it was seen there around mid-morning. This time, perseverance pays: I go back to Salthouse, and there it is, seeming ridiculously tame. Through the telescope at twenty feet, I can take down a full description of the plumage of this rather nondescript-looking bird: buffish head and breast, grey-brown back, attenuated shape with very long tertials and primaries, white belly, black legs and bill, slight eye stripe. A good rarity in spite of its unprepossessing appearance.

In the afternoon, at Cley beach, the sea is very still and shimmering. Some way out, an Arctic skua is pursuing a couple of Sandwich terns. Inshore, there are not many birds about apart from a few common terns and a pair of black terns. I return to the North Hide to get a

Spoonbills. Titchwell, Norfolk. August.

Green sandpiper and stoat. Cley,
Norfolk. August.

close look at the avocets. The whimbrels are quite active, calling and
moving from one field to another. Threatening clouds are again massing
to the west, over Blakeney. If only the deluge could obliterate the
caravan site there, it would remove the only visual scar on this lovely
stretch of coast.

Cley, 28th August
Before breakfast, from the Bittern Hide on the marshes, I observe a
few waders: spotted redshanks, curlew sandpipers, little stint and,
very close, a green sandpiper. There are a lot of bearded tits; a recep-
tion committee of five is perched on a wattle screen at the approach
to the hide. After watching for a while from the hide, I become aware
of a stoat working the margins of the pool, making quick dashes and
dancing movements, trying to attract a spotted redshank, which moves
closer but is still well out in the water – I do not know if stoats will
attempt to cross water to get their prey. The stoat transfers his atten-
tions to the green sandpiper which has by now walked round to his
patch. More dancing movements from one patch of vegetation to
another, while the sandpiper looks across occasionally and moves
closer. Then finally a lunging dive at the bird with the stoat absolutely
flat along the mud. The green sandpiper retreats hurriedly. The stoat
peers about him, stands up; his head spins round, and he departs the
scene.

Besthorpe, 3rd September
Here on an evening visit that manages to coincide with the first drop
of rain for three days, I decide to press on and am rewarded with the

Water rail. Anderby, Lincolnshire. October.

Overleaf:
Smews with goosanders. Flevoland, Holland. January.

sight of a black-tailed godwit, a rare visitor to these small pools. It is nice to find one on my own patch after having recently seen a large party in Norfolk. There are no small waders, but a greenshank, a ruff and at least fifty snipe. The swans seem to have disappeared, their favourite place having lost most of its water. The biggest influx has been of gulls: there must be about two hundred black-headed as well as quite a few larger gulls. It is hard to tell if they have been feeding on the stubble in the fields before the straw burning, or have been attracted by the new ploughing, or are breeding birds congregating before moving away.

Besthorpe, 10th September

This evening, the place is alive with birds. Masses of hirundines are gathering over the water. There are some interesting waders – ruff, greenshank, green sandpiper – and while I am watching a greenshank, I hear the call of a wood sandpiper. I find him way up in the sky and watch him plummet down, land on the mud, preen, rest and feed a bit. The fact that there is also a black tern here tonight indicates that there are at least a few easterly birds coming in. If they have got this far inland, the birdwatching must be very good on the Norfolk coast. The advanced state of the season is shown by the presence of sixty or seventy teal and a few wigeon.

Besthorpe, 18th September

It is a very warm day, with a light, southerly wind, and the waders have gone for a simple reason: no mud, no waders. The best places have been flooded for reasons to do with the gravel pit workings. As a compensation, the area is graced by three whinchats – the third autumn in a row that they have appeared here on passage, although I have never had a spring record. At the moment, they are in the haw-thorn bush that was used by the roosting corn buntings earlier in the year. A single swallow is all that remains of last week's mass of hirundines, and no terns of any sort are to be seen this week. There has been a big exodus of ducks, which has left behind a few wigeons and about the same number of teal as last week. Herons are up in numbers, including some juveniles, which is a good sign.

Besthorpe, 25th September

The water in the pits has remained quite high, and so there are still no waders. Many more ducks have come in. Although there are still the same few wigeon, there are a large number of mallard and a gadwall. About a hundred teal explode out of the marsh, flying in all directions; they will move back when I have gone. The snipe have considerably increased in numbers – there must be about seventy-five today.

Anderby, 3rd October

Earlier in the week, there was a blue-winged teal on the pits. The main Huttoft pit is crowded with coots and ducks – mallards, wigeons, shovelers and gadwall. The light is wrong for the angle from which I approach, and many teal are springing out of the reeds, so that there is little point in hunting for the blue-winged teal. In a small marshy area at Anderby Creek, I hear two water rails calling; they seem almost to be conversing. I eventually find that they are on two tiny pools, neither more than twenty by thirty feet. It is frustrating to hear their calls and not to be able to see them. Then one bird shows its head – just a suspicious red eye and a red bill are visible in the gloom among the reeds. After a while, it emerges: it swims and clambers to another part of the pool. Now I have an excellent view of it. Against the darkness of the water, the flesh-coloured legs are very much paler than I remember.

Kentish plovers. Near Fuzeta, Portugal. October.

PORTUGAL: Autumn

Black-winged stilts with black-tailed godwits, avocet and little egrets. Near Olhão, Portugal. October.

Southern Portugal, 20th October
Between Faro, which is the main town in southern Portugal and the thriving fishing village of Olhão, but actually extending beyond them in each direction, lies a vast area of sandbars and tidal flats. Apart from masses of gulls – mainly herring, with great and lesser black-backs further out on the sandbars and mudflats – some little egrets are flighting and feeding, and there are also a few Sandwich terns. When we finally find a track out into the area of lagoons, our first stop reveals some fascinating sights: quite a few black-winged stilts in small groups, an avocet, black-tailed godwits and several little egrets –

a promising start. Another track into the lagoons seems to take us to a more saline part, with low vegetation on the little islets and lining the dykes and banks. This track produces one or two egrets, a grey heron – the species found in Britain – a few crested larks and a couple of male Sardinian warblers playing a game of tag around the low bushes.

Moving further east along the coast to Fuzeta, we gain access to a large channel very similar to Blakeney harbour in Norfolk. Beyond the water is a line of sand dunes with the occasional small building. Fishing boats are plying back and forth. There is a small sandbar out in the channel; scanning that through binoculars, I find, to my delight, a Caspian tern sitting with a few herring gulls. It is a magnificent bird with a carrot-red bill, the largest of the European terns, and only the second I have seen on this side of the Atlantic – the first was at Bes-thorpe, near my home. A kingfisher streaks down the channel, turns his plumage into the sunlight, banks round some rocks and is gone in flash of brilliance. The water here must be chock-a-block with fish, which are leaping up all over the place.

Sandwich terns with mallards, cormorant, herring gulls and honey buzzards. Near Praia da Rocha, Portugal. October.

Southern Portugal, 21st October

Today, we travel west to look at the sandy cliffs with their beautiful erosion patterns and superb beaches beneath them. At Praia da Rocha, beloved of the travel industry's photographers, the beach is crowded with tourists. Venturing a little further east, we find a slightly less

Sardinian warblers. Near Olhão, Portugal. October.

Whimbrels, bar-tailed godwits, little egrets. Alvor, Portugal. October.

populous section of beach. If you gaze out to sea or along at the cliffs, the view is fabulous, but you have only to turn round and you see the bedlam of the construction business in full cry with acres of buildings in various stages of completion. We settle down on an apparently birdless beach to soak up the sun. Just offshore, though, I spot a party of about sixty mallards. A winter plumage grey wagtail comes and plays on the rocks at the edge of the surf. There are cormorants and Sandwich terns going past. A few herring gulls attach themselves loosely to the party of mallards. Out to sea are two large birds with a flopping flight; through the telescope I can see that they are honey buzzards, which is exciting even though they and the other birds here all occur in Nottinghamshire. What makes the difference is the setting.

Further west, towards the town of Alvor, is a wide river valley which we follow towards the sea, passing a field where a cloud of white birds is following a tractor. They turn out to be cattle egrets, between 120 and 130 of them – quite a change from the usual black-headed gulls. Beyond Alvor, the estuary broadens out, and the high tide has pushed the birds up to the shore. There are whimbrels, curlews, bar-tailed godwits, Kentish plovers and more little egrets.

Southern Portugal, 22nd October

We return to Praia da Rocha when the tide is further out, hoping that there will be fewer people. Although it is a gloriously sunny morning, the beach is almost empty. The sky is solid blue, the sun glints off the waves, and red and yellow colours jump out from the cliffs. The grey wagtail is here again, buzzing around our heads, slipping down to the rocks on the shore, in and out of the little curling wavelets that are rushing in. What we did not see yesterday were the crag martins which are tirelessly weaving among the hollows along the face of the cliff. A kingfisher flashes round a great bluff of cliff, sees me and heads quickly out to sea. There is much here that reminds me of my visit to Flamborough Head in July. There are similar soft rock cliffs, and the house martins and pied wagtails are replaced here on the southern tip of Europe by crag martins and wintering grey wagtails.

Our final destination is the tip of Portugal, indeed, the south-western extremity of Europe, Cape St Vincent. Like all land's ends, it is a bleak cliff area with sparse vegetation, very windswept, particularly today, when there is a strong north-westerly blowing. A short sea-watch produces a Cory's shearwater, a Manx shearwater and a steady stream of gannets in small numbers. An immature peregrine falcon drifts over the headland, apparently unaffected by the wind, plays with a herring gull, stooping at it, frightening it and then moving on. Because of the wind, there are very few small birds about – all I see is one meadow pipit and two stonechats. The continual blustering makes observation difficult, and it is too windy to leave the tripod unattended.

The bird I really want to see here is the chough. My first sortie produces nothing but a few jackdaws, and I am on the point of giving up when a cloud of birds rises out of the cliffside vegetation further along than I have explored. When we get there, we find about fifty choughs split into two parties. They are performing marvellous aerobatics in the fierce wind, planing, soaring, plummeting, at one point swept like a bundle of rags down to the bottom of the cliff, only to regain total control with a flick of the wing and emerge again into the sunlight. Often they stoop with closed wings like a raptor, but always able to return to normal flight.

Southern Portugal, 24th October

It is Sunday and the whole population of Alvor seems to make for the mudflats as soon as the tide is out, by lorry, motorcycle, car or on foot, and carrying buckets and cloths and digging implements. They soon return laden with various sorts of shellfish. This is obviously competition for the oystercatchers, which fly around calling peevishly. Among the usual gulls out on the sand, I search in vain for a Mediterranean gull. Distant sounds of shotgun fire suggest that the locals have another sort of interest in the bird population. Just before leaving, I find another Caspian tern, this time resting on the sandbar, preening and probing its plumage with its massive red bill. The little egrets

Grey wagtail with crag martins. Near Praia da Rocha, Portugal. October.

62

64

Whimbrels. Alvor, Portugal. October

seem pretty tolerant of disturbance; a cockle-gatherer has a dog with him, and they seem to delight in rushing into the shallow water and flushing the egrets.

On the edge of the mud where I am watching crabs are emerging from holes about three quarters of an inch in diameter. Very similar in size and behaviour to the fiddler crabs on the Wellfleet Marshes in Massachusetts, they sit on the surface making occasional little scurrying movements. At the sound of anything approaching, they immediately vanish *en masse*.

Southern Portugal, 25th October

On the return trip, we stop at the salt pans where we saw black-winged stilts at the start of the trip. They have gone, but there are still plenty of other birds: about twenty little egrets, a few black-tailed godwits and many redshanks, which give their usual early warning and consequently flush almost everything else. There are a few smaller waders – dunlin and ringed plover – and a great grey shrike perched on a wire near one of the small cottages.

At Olhão, the harbour is bristling with boats, just as British fishing ports must once have done. There is a tremendous gathering of herring gulls, a typical feature of any fishing port, but hardly anything else: one or two great black-backs, a Caspian tern and about twenty little egrets. Three gulls on a distant sandbar could be Mediterranean gulls, but I cannot be sure – they are just beyond the range of the telescope. One of the problems with bird-watching in the Algarve is that most of the shoreline is on an east-west axis, which means that when you look out towards the sea, you are looking southwards, into the sun, and the glittering reflections do not help long-distance identification.

At Fuzeta, the first place I saw a Caspian tern here, there are now two of them. This time, the tide is falling, exposing an increasing

Above, Caspian terns and below, Sandwich terns. Alvor, Portugal. October.

Left:
Choughs. Cape St Vincent, Portugal. October.

Caspian tern and herring gulls. Fuzeta, Portugal. October.

expanse of mud, and they are sitting out on a greenish patch in lordly isolation. On the sand bars are Sandwich terns, herring gulls and a variety of waders: curlews, bar-tailed godwits, grey plovers, knots and turnstones. A small pool near the village of Fuzeta is full of waders, mainly redshanks, with over forty Kentish plovers, plus dunlins and ringed plovers. It is another cloudless day, with a faint breeze on the beaches, but really hot in the towns. The local people are wearing cardigans, while the British in the resorts are happiest with their clothes off.

Further east, between the town of Tavira and the shore, is another good area of saltpans with egrets as usual, quite a few black-tailed godwits and black-winged stilts and, perhaps the best bird of the trip, a white stork, which is busily preening. Waders include a little stint, the first I have seen here, dunlins, sanderlings, ringed plovers, redshanks, spotted redshanks, greenshanks and a curlew sandpiper. Two kingfishers flash past.

We end by searching local woods without success for azure-winged magpies, but we do find a waxbill, a small finch-like species that has apparently been introduced into Portugal from Africa, as well as firecrests, serins, Sardinian warblers, various leaf warblers and a black redstart.

White stork. Tavira, Portugal. October.

BRITAIN: Winter

ENGLAND

Besthorpe, 6th November

The sort of grey day that seems to characterise November. I arrive to find dozens of fieldfares erupting from hedges that are still laden with berries, although the leaves are disappearing fast. Redwings stream overhead, their thin calls emerging from the gloom. I look around hopefully in case a shrike has drifted in with this influx.

There are ducks in quantity. One pool holds most of the surface feeders: about ninety wigeons, twenty-five shovelers and about 270 mallards. The diving ducks are represented by thirty pochards, thirty tufted ducks and three goosanders – a male, a female and an immature male. There are five gadwalls feeding with the wigeon. The family of mute swans has stayed together, and the two adults and four young are all asleep in a corner of a pit. A short-eared owl leaps out from the grassy bank of one of the dry pits, turns in the air and gives me a lingering, rather annoyed look over his shoulder as he goes off to another part of the gravel workings. The marshy area is full of snipe and teal – probably about a hundred snipe and seventy to eighty teal. I flush a jack snipe among them, and later flush another one from an isolated pool.

Anderby Creek, Lincolnshire, 7th November

I have come to see if any migrants are lingering here. I am told that there was a yellow-browed warbler here earlier in the week, but there is no sign of it now. As I walk among almost leafless sycamores beside a mass of sea buckthorn, a small bird flies in front of me. It could be a song thrush or a redwing. Certainly, it is smaller than the blackbirds which are everywhere here. Looking through the binoculars at the spot where it has flown into the vegetation reveals a red tail, which suggests that it may be a redstart, but then I see the size of the whole bird, which is definitely too large, and realise that it is a rarity, a shrike of a red-tailed variety from Eastern Europe and Asia, one of those that used to be classed as subspecies of the red-backed shrike. This particular bird has the characteristics of the Isabelline shrike, which is now recognised as a full species. The crown, nape and back are greybrown – looking very grey in some lights – with a black face mask, pale supercilium and dark, hooked bill. The wings are dark, with a small square of white at the base of the primaries and pale edges to the tertials. The tail, orangey red above and below, is raised and lowered constantly. The breast and underparts are pale buff with a pinkish wash, shading paler to almost white on the chin. I have two very good views of it before it vanishes into very thick cover – typical shrike behaviour. I shall remember for a long time the moment when I first saw its grey back and red tail and it turned its head to reveal the black facial mask.

At Chapel Pits, I see a long-tailed duck at very close range – a female or immature bird. There are a few other things about: Brent geese flying over, larks, lapwings and gulls in the fields. I search for the shrike again without success, but flush a woodcock, a typical late autumn migrant to this coast. Later, three pintails fly through over the sea to the south.

Isabelline shrike. Anderby Creek, Lincolnshire. November.

Gibraltar Point, Lincolnshire, 8th November

After the Isabelline shrike yesterday, I had a late evening telephone call to say that an even rarer bird, an American redstart, had turned up at Gibraltar Point. Today, it is still there, a little American wood warbler with a distinctive yellow patch on the front of the wing and beautiful yellow markings above and below the tail. The two remarkable sightings within twenty-four hours highlight the excitement of migration watching on the coast. On this small section of the Lincolnshire shore, vagrants from Asia and America have arrived almost simultaneously both having come great distances from their place of origin. After an initial view, the American redstart disappears and there is a miserable hour during which a lot of people leave and only a few stay in the hope of relocating the bird. This is a typical occurrence when you are looking for migrants. You think the bird has gone, and a general gloom settles until, as in this case, a call is heard and the bird reappears. For the next three-quarters of an hour, we have superb views as it flits in and out of the hawthorn bushes. It flicks and spreads its tail, showing the great yellow patches. Tinges of orange to the yellow of the breast indicate that it is an immature male. Everybody who has stayed has had a terrific morning. Other people have gone off towards Anderby in search of the Isabelline shrike, armed with hastily drawn sketch maps. It is good to be one bird ahead of the crowd – a rare occurrence for me.

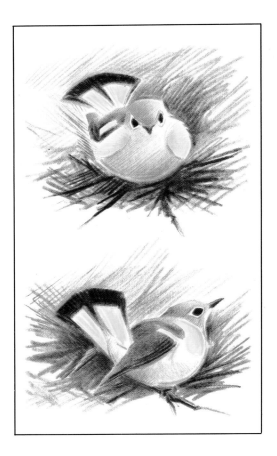

American redstart. Gibraltar Point, Lincolnshire. November.

Winthorpe, 15th November

I hear that the Isabelline shrike has reappeared today at Gibraltar Point. At dusk, it was apparently sighted in the same bush as the American redstart.

Besthorpe, 27th November

Last night, we had the first good frost of the autumn. Much of the shallower water has a thin film of ice, which has displaced the snipe. As the sunny day begins to fade into the cool stillness of a wintery afternoon, I see the short-eared owl hunting along the fringes of one of the pools, moving gracefully and quietly. The few sounds that there are seem magnified in the stillness of the day, and the regular calls of the teal in the reeds sound like the creaking of ice. Just as the day is drawing to an end, I hear a familiar but unexpected call. It is a beautiful male bearded tit, illuminated by the last rays of the sun as it climbs up some reedmace, so that I can see the blue-grey colour of its head and its black moustache. It calls several times and then disappears. This is the first bearded tit that I have seen in the Midlands, although in general they are relatively plentiful at the moment and there have been quite a number in Lincolnshire. Nevertheless, it is a splendid bird to find in Nottinghamshire.

Stone Creek, North Humberside, 30th November

I have had news of a green heron here, just to the east of Hull. As I saw several dozen of these birds in the United States in May, I have come to view the first live record of the species in Britain. The only other record was a dead specimen identified years later from a collection in Cornwall. At first, the bird is in a little tidal pool against the sun and is just a moribund-looking black blob, but as the sun comes round and the bird can be watched under better conditions, it becomes more active. It catches several fish and starts striding purposefully around the little grass hummocks beside the pool. With full sunlight playing on it against a translucent background of the River Humber and its

Green heron. Stone Creek, North
Humberside. November.

Bearded tit. Besthorpe,
Nottinghamshire. November.

ghostly ships sailing through the haze, I can see the subtlety of its
colours – the blue-grey of the back and the dark green wing feathers,
each defined by its buff edging. There are two pale streaks on the
warm, rich brown of the breast; the eye is hard and mean, with a
yellow patch beside it; the bill is orange with a yellowish tip, and the
legs are also orange. There has also been a great white heron in the
area, but that has moved on today and denied me the pleasure of two
exceptional birds in a day. However, the green heron is something to
relish and a fitting close to a superb month for rare birds.

Besthorpe, 1st January

The fresh westerly wind blowing across the pits is an ideal wakener
from New Year hangovers. Ducks are plentiful: 120 teal and 150
wigeon as well as the odd goosander and shoveler. The number of
snipe is up to about eighty. A sparrowhawk passes through. A small
strip of exposed mud on the edge of the marshy area holds five ruffs
and then four redshanks. I work hard at trying to find a jack snipe,
but have no luck – perhaps it is too wet for them, as the muddy patches
that they like are submerged.

The weather is too mild to produce much diversity in the winter
birds. It needs a good cold snap for everything to move around, and
perhaps to bring some immigration from Europe.

Harwich, 13th January

A good day to set out by ferry across the North Sea. The water of the
Stour estuary is grey and brown, sparkling a little under the brightening
sky. About fifty Brent geese fly up the river, and so, later, do parties
of waders – knots and dunlins. As the ferry moves out into open
water, we start seeing kittiwakes, which appear with increasing reg-
ularity, mostly adults, with a few immature birds. I spot three divers,
one of them definitely a red-throated, as well as guillemots in ones
and twos, in both winter and summer plumage. The North Sea looks
rather benign for January, with a blue sky and grey clouds over calm
water. A small trawler comes into view surrounded by a cloud of
gulls, which seem to envelop the whole boat, with a great mass of
them at the stern. Among them are a number of gannets. One or two
fulmars appear, but except when trawlers pass, the bird life tails off.
Occasionally, we see little parties of kittiwakes. Ten of them settle in
front of us, as delicately as butterflies, on the bank of a wave.

HOLLAND: Winter

Flevoland, 14th January

Flevoland is the great polder of reclaimed land to the north-east of Amsterdam. It is highly landscaped, with everything in its place and doing a job – the canals are laid out and the fields and woods planted with precision. We drive around and locate a very large flock of geese – our estimates vary up to about three thousand – principally white-fronts with about two hundred barnacle geese mixed in. They are perhaps a little too distant for really good views. On one of the fields, we find about seventy-five bean geese, hardly standing out against the greyish brown of the earth. In a short space of time, we come across two ring-tail hen harriers flying low over grass fields; one of them settles close enough for us to see the facial mask and markings. The weather, which is already gloomy, worsens as the drizzle turns into snow and visibility deteriorates. A rather distant rough-legged buzzard hovers long enough to show its white tail with black terminal band before it vanishes into some trees. We work our way to the town of Lelystad, where there are large coastal pools which are the haunt of smew. Initially we cannot see much through the horizontal snow, but we manage to make out about fifty smews and a similar number of goosanders. In one corner, well out of the wind, is a huge pack of pochards and tufted ducks, probably two thousand of them. There are several hooded crows, two of which are perched on a small island where they are joined by a heron. Great crested grebes are numerous both on the Ijsselmeer and on the lakes, where a pair near the smews are competing with each other in display even though they are still in winter plumage. As we work west along the north coast of Flevoland, there are vast number of pochards and tufted ducks. Among them is a single male long-tailed duck; one or two scaups are possibly flying further out, but we cannot make a positive identification.

The great marsh on the north-west side of the polder, the Oost-vaardersplassen, is a huge expanse about six miles long with reed beds and patches of open water. Even in the driving rain, we spot a rough-legged buzzard with the whiteness of its tail emerging from the browns and yellows. Towards the end of the day, the weather relents briefly, and a burst of sunshine produces great raptor activity: sparrowhawks,

Hen harriers, buzzard. Flevoland, Holland. January.

Hooded crows. Flevoland, Holland. January.

Slavonian grebe and tufted ducks.
Flevoland, Holland. January.

Overleaf:
Wheatear, Kentish plover, avocets,
whimbrel, dunlins. Noirmoutier,
France. April.

several kestrels, four marsh harriers, a larger number of hen harriers
and quite a few buzzards are all wheeling around, mainly over the
great marsh, where they fly among the sallow bushes. A female hen
harrier dances with a male. On a roadside pool at the edge of the marsh
is a small group of avocets.

Flevoland, 15th January

The weather is poor again, with lashing rain, but ornithologically the
day starts well, with a Slavonian grebe in winter plumage seen from
the causeway between Harderwijk and Flevoland. As we progress
across the island, buzzards are regularly to be seen, and we find three
hen harriers in one spot. As we stop to identify some redwings in a
wood, a sparrowhawk flies in, selects a victim and takes it as it tries to
get back into the trees. The succession of road-side buzzards provides
a chance to see how diverse their plumage is – one spectacular bird
seems to be creamy white all over. As we reach the edge of the great

71

Rough-legged buzzards with marsh and
hen harriers. Flevoland, Holland.
January.

Rough-legged buzzards. Flevoland, Holland. January.

marsh, two rough-legged buzzards are hanging in the wind beside the road, and we are able to drive almost underneath them, our first really excellent view of these birds. They are joined by a female hen harrier, which stays with them for a while and then leaves. The rough-legged buzzards momentarily grip talons in the air and tumble down, then part and fly away. On the lake nearby are a few pintails.

At the Oostvaardersplassen, we take the boardwalk out to the *vogelhut* or hide. In common with many another hide, the vista it offers contains no birds, just a great expanse of water. At the smew lake, however, we find the whole population of smew out in the open, a total of about 250 (not quite the numbers we had hoped for), including a large flock of 200 with 84 drakes in it. At the back, is a supporting cast of about 120 goosanders.

We leave Flevoland over the northern bridge and work our way round to Urk, where we are lucky enough to discover a huge flock of at least 1,500 bean geese, plus seven Bewick's swans, including two young birds, and two adult snow geese. One can only conjecture about the origin of the snow geese: perhaps they are genuine transatlantic vagrants, but they are more likely to have escaped from wildfowl collections. Driving back down the eastern side of Flevoland, we pass an endless mass of tufted ducks and pochards for the whole length of the drive. The numbers of wildfowl here are really incredible.

Flevoland, 16th January

We start by rewarding ourselves with a brief respite from the lashing that we have been taking from the elements on the marsh and coast. We spend a few hours in the forest south of Harderwijk where we make two excellent sightings of goshawks, as well as seeing crested tits, short-toed treecreepers, sparrowhawks, great spotted woodpecker and sundry other woodland birds. Then we head back to the smew pool near Lelystad. As it is Sunday, quite a lot of Dutch birdwatchers are out. The numbers of smew are slightly reduced. On the coast, the duck population has greatly diminished – perhaps in better weather, like today's, they go somewhere else. We note a fine continental race cormorant with a white head. Just before we reach the Oostvaardersplassen marsh, we see a big party of whooper swans, and a roe deer in a field.

Pochards, tufted ducks, cormorant. Flevoland, Holland. January.

We return to the smew pool to find that there are windsurfers on it and the ducks have been driven away to the main lake on the other side of the road, where it is much more difficult to watch them. Towards evening, the congregation of crows (mainly hooded) in the woods increases, reaching several hundred. As dusk falls, with a wide band of red sky above the marsh, hundreds of geese pour in, probably to roost on the lake. Starlings, too, are going to their roosts and more crows arrive in another area of woodland. When we drive away, we catch a short-eared owl in the car headlights and get a point-blank view of it perching among the roadside grass.

Hook of Holland, 17th January

As the ferry moves out, we note about a dozen purple sandpipers on a breakwater made of gigantic rectangular blocks of concrete. A bit further out, we see an adult little gull in the distance and three scoters flying past. Once the ferry is on the open sea, we get one or two auks, mainly guillemots, then several razorbills, plus kittiwakes and just a few gannets. It is a further hour before there is the excitement of a bonxie or great skua *en route* for a gull-enshrouded fishing trawler, a strong bird, making its way powerfully over the waves at the stern of the boat and then lingering with some adult gannets.

BRITAIN: Winter-Spring

ENGLAND

Besthorpe, 23rd January

Although the wind is cold, the weather is not bad for late January. The mute swan family is still faithful to its breeding pool. The four young have now grown as big as their parents. Their necks have become creamy white, their bodies are blotched pale brown and greyish white, and they have little dark caps to their heads. Ten goosanders take off, strung out in a line, and depart to quieter water. In the background is the sound of wigeons whistling. The main pool holds about two hundred mallards, with three shelducks and a couple of great crested grebes. Some fifty teal leave their marshy patch and work the sky before finding a resting place.

I can now see that there is another pair of swans on the other side of the marsh from the family group. They are indulging in a vocal exchange, whether to discuss me or territorial rights on the pools, I'm not sure. The family take off with heavy beating of wings as they become airborne. They circle and come down on the same pool as the intruding pair. The landing is quite spectacular – as two of the young overshoot the landing spot but draw back into the family group. The two adults, side by side, with wings raised and necks right back so that their heads are between their wings, advance solidly right up to the intruding pair, who give way, turning and taking flight towards the pool vacated by the family. Things seem to have been sorted out, but, as I leave, the adult male of the family decides to continue the vendetta on his own and flies over to the other pool to intimidate the pair.

Clumber Park, Nottinghamshire, 30th January

The benign weather gave me a very dull afternoon of birdwatching yesterday at Besthorpe and South Muskham pits. Today, I have come to Clumber Park, which covers some 3,800 acres of the ancient Sherwood Forest. Almost immediately, I am rewarded by seeing a party of four or five hawfinches, which sit warily in the tree tops, waiting for me to leave. By the edge of the lake is a nice little marshy pool, full of mossy logs and fringed with the green of rhododendron leaves under a towering cathedral of wintery trees. Approaching from a direction that I have not tried before, I catch a water rail out in the open; he freezes, and I have a fine view of him before he takes fright and bolts like a rodent into the cover of the rhododendrons.

South Muskham, 12th February

A sprinkling of snow makes the place look wintery. Apart from the small resident bunch of tufted ducks and pochards, there are about thirty-two great crested grebes, with three or four pairs in various stages of courtship. My star bird today is a single ruddy duck – the first time I have seen one in Nottinghamshire.

Girton, 12th February

I have come here after an uneventful early afternoon at Besthorpe, where there was the depressing sight of someone ripping up vegetation with an excavator, removing the birds' feeding and nesting places. At the gull roost, I find a disappointing number of large gulls

Mediterranean gull and black-headed gulls. Girton, Nottinghamshire. February.

– just a few great black-backs – and turn my attention to the main flock of black-headeds. Scanning through them, I am thrilled to see an adult Mediterranean gull, just coming out of its winter plumage. The head is dusky, with a concentration of black around the eye and a much heavier deep red bill than that of a black-headed. At a distance, the wings have a blunt-ended appearance because of the white wing tips. It is a remarkable bird to see in the middle of England and for me a personal first away from the coast.

South Muskham, 18th February

A brief evening visit to look at the gull roost. After about a quarter of an hour, the gulls are disturbed. I drive off to the pool by the A1, and see a black-throated diver in winter plumage swimming and diving near the edge of the water. The gulls have not returned, but I can see fifty-nine great crested grebes, the most I have ever seen in Nottinghamshire. The gulls still seem quite disturbed: they have made as if to return to the pool I first looked at, but have come back and scattered in various directions, some by the sugar beet factory, others on the fields. There is no point in searching for a glaucous gull tonight.

Gibraltar Point, 20th February

This is my first visit here since the excitement of the American redstart in November. Some twites are feeding near a creek. I watch them for a while and then walk out to the shore. The sea is very calm and grey, with just a ripple of waves moving in. Very close to the shore are red-throated divers in winter plumage being so active that it is hard to assess exactly how many there are. Eight fly in and land just offshore, where they preen and swim, doing their characteristic belly roll to preen their undersides.

The shore itself is very quiet. At first, there are only grey plovers about, but then a few sanderlings appear, coming down the beach. Finally, about twenty snow buntings arrive and mingle with the sanderlings, forming a party. Later, we find the remains of a sanderling, just a leg and a wing, but the leg has a ring on it. It was probably killed by a merlin. [When the ring is sent to the British Trust for Ornithology, we learn that the bird was ringed at Heacham in Norfolk on 31st March 1968.]

Anderby, 20th February

We search the beach for casualties after reports of a large auk wreck. There are many dead razorbills, most of them adults, a few guillemots,

Little auk corpse. Anderby, Lincolnshire. February.

two puffins and the remains of three little auks, all in the space of about eight hundred yards. It seems sad that these birds of the oceans end by becoming beach debris in Lincolnshire. Many of the razorbills have pristine plumage, but others, obviously longer dead, are just carcases. As we return to the car, a short-eared owl appears, hunting along the grassy verges and the roadside ditch.

Besthorpe, 26th February

I can feel warm air on my face as I leave the car. Skylarks are singing and a lapwing is tumbling in the sky. There are very few ducks left, but three pairs of shelducks are starting their courtship, cackling and flying around. A flight of sixteen shovelers and a few teal goes past. It is good to hear the cries of the golden plovers echoing around the fields. As I walk along the dried out bank, there is a sudden eruption of birds: two herons, a shelduck and two short-eared owls all pop out of the bank. There are now about five pairs of shelducks in all here.

Besthorpe, 5th March

Strong westerly winds are scouring the Trent Valley. There are a few ducks, mainly in the lee of the banks. Half a dozen goldeneyes are out on the rough water – will they decide to leave as I approach? They decide to leave. The two short-eared owls are in their favourite corner as the gale howls. They rise into the wind, hang there and then drift away backwards, watching me.

Gibraltar Point, 6th March

I have come back to get some more material for the painting of divers, sanderlings and snow buntings that I started planning on my last visit. My first good sighting, though, is of a merlin coming in low over the dunes, down over the marsh, past the information centre and away, making a superb stoop, probably on some skylarks, as it goes. Perhaps this bird was the assassin of the sanderling whose ring we removed a fortnight ago. Apart from the merlins, the birds are much the same as last time, but without any good views of the divers. Although the finer weather has brought more people to disturb the beach, I still manage to see as much as I need of the sanderlings and snow buntings for the painting.

Sanderlings and snow buntings with red-throated divers. Gibraltar Point, Lincolnshire. February.

SCOTLAND

Loch Fleet, Sutherland, 12th March

Although Loch Fleet is tidal, it is connected to the sea only by quite a narrow channel. The tide is coming in, but a lot of mud is still exposed in the tidal basin. There is only a scattering of birds – a few mergansers, one or two eiders and oystercatchers – and so we move out to the shore near Embo. There are not as many ducks here as I had hoped. In the middle distance are a good number of scoters, including some velvet scoters, whose white wing patches are visible as they fly over the sea. There are small groups of eiders where it is rocky, and I scan them for the king eider which I know has been with them in previous winters. Among the few long-tailed ducks are one or two splendid males as well as the drab females and immatures.

Further south round Embo Bay from the pier, a group of velvet scoters is close enough for us to see the white markings by the eyes and the yellow sides to the bills. They are strong birds, much stronger than common scoters, and surge through the water with their necks erect. As the tide comes in, the waders are pushed back to the rocks, with the white foam close behind them. We come across a party of turnstones, three purple sandpipers, grey plovers and curlews. A small group of twites appears on the beach. The parties of both sorts of scoter are scattered widely over the sea, and any binocular field of view must contain twenty or thirty birds, a lot of them in the distance. We search them quite thoroughly for possible vagrant surf scoters, but the number of birds, many on the edge of our visual range, makes the task virtually impossible. There is a great northern diver out in the bay, some distance away but quite recognisable because of its shape and large size. At the mouth of Loch Fleet are many more eiders: at one side there is a party of 158 and there are more on the other, but still no king eider – we must keep looking.

Loch Fleet, 13th March

A calm, sunny morning with the sea glistening beneath a broken sky. Much the same pattern of birds as yesterday, and again we search unsuccessfully for the king eider. With high tide at ten o'clock, the eiders from the mouth of Loch Fleet have moved further out to sea.

Purple sandpipers and turnstones. Embo, Sutherland (Highland region). March.

Long-tailed ducks and eiders. Loch Fleet, Sutherland (Highland region). March.

Low tide is clearly the best time for watching them. The waders are also much the same as yesterday, with the addition of a single bar-tailed godwit.

Wick, Caithness, 13th March

A Ross's gull was seen here last weekend, and we have travelled north on the chance that it might still be around. There have also been both sorts of large white-winged gulls, and we have the possibility of seeing them as well. Almost as soon as we arrive, we find two glaucous gulls, one in its first winter and one in its second, and two similarly plumaged Iceland gulls. In the harbour, there are also about twenty-five golden-eyes and several black guillemots. Just one of the white-winged gulls stays around, the second-winter Iceland. We resort to throwing bread to tempt it closer and earn ourselves close-up views – creamy white plumage with delicate, lace-like brown markings and just the primaries completely white. A red-throated diver appears in the harbour, as does a long-tailed duck close to the black guillemots. As the tide recedes and the mud is exposed, the gull activity rises to a frenzy – they feed, rise and drop to feed again. Waders are passing through all the time, mainly turnstones, but also purple sandpipers – thirty-one of them so far. Jackdaws are mingling with the gulls on the mud. There are now forty goldeneyes which look spectacular with the sunlight picking out the bottle green of the drakes' heads and the gold of the females' eyes; some of their bills have little gold tips.

Loch Fleet, 14th March

Another placid morning, with the sea an oily silver colour. There is something of a swell, which makes continuous observation difficult; the birds appear and disappear all the time, particularly if they are diving as well. The eiders, about 170 this time, are at the mouth of

Iceland gulls, goldeneyes, black guillemots. Wick, Caithness (Highland region). March.

Velvet scoters. Embo, Sutherland (Highland region). March.

Loch Fleet, but there is still no sign of the king eider. They move out to sea, in and out of the rough water, and suddenly they are all in flight. Small groups land on the water and move back into the loch on the rushing tide. A group of males with one or two females play and croon as they are carried along. A great northern diver is feeding at the mouth of the loch, often holding his head under water to work on his prey. Some way out are four Slavonian grebes with their rather distinctive shape, silvery white breast and white face patch, but already with the red summer colour on the neck – that early March stage when they can be confused with red-necked grebes. One or two ringed plovers on the beach are already setting up territories on the flatter, stony expanses. One black-throated and two red-throated divers mean that we have seen all three common species in a single morning.

At Embo, there is still no king eider among the usual pattern of small eider parties. I pan my telescope over the whole flock of scoters which is spread out across the sea. There is a preponderance now of velvets, with more males than females, but we have a fine, close view of a female and can see the double pale disc pattern on the cheeks. The drake velvets are superb, with sooty black plumage and the bright sunlight catching the white eye flecks and the bright yellow of the bill.

ENGLAND

Short-eared owl. Besthorpe, Nottinghamshire. April.

Besthorpe, 27th March

Recent promises of spring have been abruptly halted by a cold north-easterly wind and drizzle. No spring migrants have arrived yet, but the golden plover flock has increased to about two hundred birds; northern birds, already in their fine summer plumage, strut among the southern birds that still look moth-eaten and dowdy. There are nineteen goosanders, ten shovelers, two pairs of gadwall, four ruffs and a few redshanks. The pair of short-eared owls is still here. The biggest surprise is the reappearance of a male bearded tit in the patch of reedmace where I saw one last November. Is it the same bird, and has he been here all winter? As I have come here several times since I last saw him, I would expect to have seen or heard something of him.

Besthorpe, 5th April

Easter Tuesday: a fine, cool evening with not a breath of wind. The most conspicuous sound is the song of the redshanks. Most of the duck have now gone, although a few diving ducks remain: one drake and several duck goosanders and a party of eleven goldeneyes. As I stand on the edge of an old, filled-in pit, one of the short-eared owls flies straight at me, apparently not having seen me. He grows in the field of the binoculars until he is just a head with bright orange eyes and pencil-thin lines of wings. He pitches, gazes at me and is away. A cock pheasant runs past, agitated by his presence. Scattered equidistantly about a nearby field are the four juvenile swans from last year, a small group of great black-back gulls, a few wood pigeons and eight pairs of mallards. As I peer over the bank at them, only the mallards' heads are showing, and they look like slightly embarrassed courting couples. The song of a curlew is added to those of the redshanks and skylarks as it patrols and displays over its favourite Trentside field. The conditions are perfect for jack snipe today, and I spot a single bird, my first record for this year. Until now, the place has usually been either frozen or too wet – jack snipe like things to be just right. There are still no migrants, but two Canada geese have just started nesting, and at dusk an excited group of snipe puts on a fine aerial display. Two corn buntings are at their roosting spot.

FRANCE: Spring

Noirmoutier, 9th April

The island of Noirmoutier is south-west of Nantes and south from the mouth of the River Loire. It is a pleasant spot with pine woods and very lush, green areas of marsh. The saline ponds and large salt pans provide a combination of shallow water and mud that is ideal for waders; their edges are overgrown and grassy, and the tangled vegetation of the bank system between them makes good cover for small birds. Much of the island is arable land, but the smallholdings and tiny farms seem in danger of being overrun by holiday cottages and camp sites. As you walk through what seems like an unspoilt wood,

Stonechat with avocets. Noirmoutier, France. April.

Bluethroat with Montagu's harriers.
Noirmoutier, France. April.

you realise that every other tree has a mark on it showing where a
tent will be pitched in the summer.

It has now been raining continuously for twenty-four hours – the
product of a vigorous depression coming in off the Atlantic – and the
place looks less than inviting. Even so, a quick drive around produces
little egrets and black-winged stilts, a green sandpiper obviously on
migration, a stonechat, an assortment of pipits and finally, in the
evening, a party of about forty avocets arriving over the salt pans.

Fan-tailed warblers, Cetti's warbler,
blue-headed wagtail, bluethroats.
Noirmoutier, France. April.

Noirmoutier, 10th April

This morning, I am working the area of old salt pans that runs from the town of Noirmoutier towards the coast of the Baie de Bourgneuf. At first, there is not much to be seen: a few avocets and two black-winged stilts. A couple of decoy ducks suggest one use to which the area is put. A garden warbler, several willow warblers and a chiffchaff are all singing. The strong wind that has replaced the rain does not help me in locating small bird noises. However, the zit-zit call of the fan-tailed warbler is coming faintly from a marsh. It gets louder and eventually I catch sight of it, a tiny, very active bird that zips up in the air, zooms about and then returns to the vegetation – it is very difficult to get a proper look at it when it is perching, but once or twice I glimpse the characteristic cocked tail. A Cetti's warbler gives occasional blasts of song from the dense brambles and tamarisks beside the salt pans. Extremely smart stonechats are visible all the time. At some distance, I notice a bird that could possibly be a bluethroat, but almost as soon as I have it in the field of the telescope, it vanishes and a little later a stonechat appears in the same place. However, I now have another darkish bird in view through the telescope and it is indeed a bluethroat, the species that I have been most hoping to see on this trip. It is absolutely resplendent – the throat is brilliant blue with a sharp white spot; the chestnut gorget is separated from the blue by a black band; the underside is white; there is a pale eye stripe and red and black on the tail. I have seen many bluethroats before on the Norfolk coast during their autumn migration. Fairly good specimens pass through in early August, but I have never seen anything remotely like this.

In the afternoon, we cover the area of salt pans from the town of Noirmoutier south to L'Epine. The weather is improving, with the sun breaking through, but still with a strong wind from the north. Again there are a few egrets, black-winged stilts and avocets as well as a redshank. Corn buntings seem to be as common as stonechats, and we see several more bluethroats. They appear in places that I would not expect, where there is only low vegetation. One of the few salt pans with any mud in it holds about thirty ringed plovers and the same number of dunlins, many of them in spring plumage. An adjacent pool has a small gathering of little gulls: nine, of which two are immature; the rest are adults just coming out of winter plumage, with pale grey hood shapes and the winter facial markings still visible. Their dainty, dipping flight sometimes makes them look almost as if they are walking on the water. They work their way across the pool against the wind as they feed, then flick into the air, letting the wind push them back so that they can work their way across again. Their pearly upper parts contrast with the black underwings as they bank into the wind. There are also white wagtails and a blue-headed wagtail; a female marsh harrier flies through.

Noirmoutier, 11th April

After another stormy night, the day has started with strong north-westerly winds bringing, as they usually do, periods of blue sky and sun. The avocets on the salt pans are as skittish and nervous as ever – they probably suffer occasional persecution here. The woods are buzzing with serins, and a Cetti's warbler, one of about three in the area, is singing away near the edge of the water.

In the afternoon, we move to the end of the road that connects the island of Noirmoutier to the mainland – like the causeway between Holy Island and Northumberland, it is passable only at low tide. With the tide coming in, a superb collection of waders is massing as the

Sandwich terns with juveniles and black-headed gulls. Blakeney Point, Norfolk. July.

water corners them. From the car, I can see a whimbrel and about twenty avocets, much closer than I managed to get to those on the salt pans; further away is a large gathering of oystercatchers beside the water and, on another sandbank, an equal number of grey plovers, only two of which are in really fine summer plumage. Out there are also a collection of knots and a few bar-tailed godwits. Between the avocets and the more distant waders, many dunlins are scattered across the mud, with ringed plovers and a small sprinkling of Kentish plovers among them. Nearest to the car, a male wheatear stands out in sharp relief against the dark wrack. This corner by the causeway is as fine a demonstration as you could want of the richness of inter-tidal mud as a feeding habitat for birds.

Bouin (Vendée), 12th April

As the causeway road from Noirmoutier to the mainland is not pass-able, we leave the island by the bridge and go a few kilometres north to look at the Bouin marshes, an area of land that was reclaimed a long time ago and is now intensively farmed – not surprisingly, it reminds me of Holland. There are no rough areas for birds, but at the northern end of the marsh, where a small river feeds into the Baie de Bourgneuf, things are much better. Running along the whole edge of the marsh is a sea wall with plenty of rough cover – tamarisks and brambles – beside it, and a wide ditch with reeds. On the extensive mudflats of the bay itself are fifty to sixty avocets feeding with shel-ducks. Bluethroats are moving about on the top of the wall, cocking their tails and singing. Their song often has an element of mimicry; one of them here includes the sounds of a bearded tit in its performance.

We have seen only a few hirundines in the past few days, but now that the weather is better, swallows and sand martins are more in evidence, passing on their way north. Their numbers are increasing all the time. When I look down the length of the bank, there seems to be a cloud of them flying in and out the bushes to pick up insects. A blue-headed wagtail perches high in the bushes, and leaf warblers creep about among the branches. A hoopoe flies right overhead, seeming to hang momentarily in the air above us. Three marsh harriers and a kestrel are hunting over the marshes.

Lac de Grand-Lieu (Loire-Atlantique), 13th April

Surrounded by reeds, sallow thickets and woods, all to various degrees impenetrable, this large lake south-west of Nantes is difficult to get at. Our vantage point, the lakeside village of Passay, seems initially to be the one place from which we can see the open water. What we immediately notice is a black kite circling around the edge of the water; in fact, we are able to count four or five in the immediate vicin-ity, while others appear as specks in the distance. There are also marsh

Little gulls. Noirmoutier, France. April.
Right:
Cirl bunting with black kites. Lac de Grand-Lieu (Loire-Atlantique), France. April.
Below:
Black kites, marsh harriers, Montagu's harriers, hoopoe. Lac du Grand-Lieu (Loire-Atlantique) and Noirmoutier, France. April.

harriers – I can see a male bringing a reed to a female who is sitting on the ground, an early stage of courtship. A few grey herons are flying or standing motionless at the edges of small reed beds. Cetti's and sedge warblers are singing and there are swifts to be seen. Where a lane leads down to the edge of the lake, we find a pair of cirl buntings, a species that I have seen only rarely in Britain. The surrounding farmland, their usual habitat, is flooded by the lake, which has risen above its normal level.

Back on the island of Noirmoutier, on the road near La Guérinière, we spot a fine male Montagu's harrier and are able to watch this most delicate of all harriers as it beats and harries in and out of the ditches and around the fields. During the evening, at Le Sableau, I sight two hoopoes, which have probably come in over the last day or two. This morning, as we left the island by the Fromentine bridge, there was one newly arrived and perched on the parapet. On the saline are four little egrets and about seventy dunlins, which are briefly disturbed when a whimbrel lands near them.

Noirmoutier, 14th April

At Le Sableau in the morning, nothing new appears, but I finally get a good, if brief, look at a Cetti's warbler and see a nice display from a fan-tailed warbler; it is back-lit and looks like a ball of dandelion fluff. Stonechats and bluethroats seem ever-present – it is surprising how dark and ominous a bluethroat can seem in a low intensity of light, when it is dazzlingly colourful in bright daylight. Crossing the Fromentine bridge, we see two more hoopoes; it seems to be a regular place for them.

On the rooftops at the beach of L'Epine, we find a female black redstart and a pair of wheatears. At low tide, we examine the intertidal rocks and weed for waders; we find three curlews, a lone common sandpiper and a large number of local people, who turn up garbed in anything from beachwear to thigh waders and special clothing to collect any shellfish they can find. At La Guérinière, the Montagu's harrier is on the same fields as before, and soon a second bird appears. Within five minutes of each other, they beat their way towards us along the edge of the track and pass within ten feet of the car. Their yellow eyes with tiny black pupils seem to gaze into the car but to see no danger – no wonder they fall victim to shotguns as they migrate over France. It is great to get so near such scarce birds, and while we are watching them at close range, we see another pair high in the sky behind them. There is a fifth bird over on the salines towards L'Epine. Driving along a small lane towards Le Sableau, I come across a hoopoe contentedly taking a dust bath.

BRITAIN: Spring–Autumn

ENGLAND

Besthorpe, 23rd April

One of the short-eared owls is lingering on here, still hunting, but will depart soon for a moorland summer. The summer migrants have arrived: sedge and willow warblers are singing, cuckoos are calling, and swallows and sand martins have arrived, although not yet in the numbers that we saw in France. A sprinkling of yellow wagtails are sharply outlined against the churned sepia earth. A solitary common tern rests on a stump out on the marsh, quietly observing the shelducks displaying. The short-eared owl reappears, and the party of yellow wagtails rises from the ground to harass him. The golden plovers have gone, apart from one northern bird, which is glorious in its summer dress, with jet black face and belly.

Besthorpe, 30th April

Coming down the lane, I am greeted by a whitethroat and a lesser whitethroat, evidently newly arrived; they sing for a short while and then move on, working their way through the high willows and the hawthorn hedges. There are a few waders this week: two common sandpipers, two dunlins and a little ringed plover, my first record for this year and much later than usual. The short-eared owl is still here. Its daylight vision must be rather poor – I can get quite close to it as it sits on a mound of earth. Later, I see it high in the sky, moving away to the south and conducting an aerial battle with two carrion crows.

Shropshire-Herefordshire border, 7th May

The River Teme is an old haunt. It seems to be a good year for common sandpipers – they fly displaying over the river, scything and flicking across the water and their piping call builds into silvery song. The Water Board has had a good time vandalising the surroundings of the river in the name of improvement. However, enough is probably left for the place to remain a good habitat for birds.

A moorhens' nest with four eggs is at the base of an alder tree on the river bank. As usual, there are dippers, one on the bridge, and one on the weir, scolding us as we approach its nest – clearly, there are young in it. I see the dipper clinging to its nest, apparently hanging by one leg above the raging torrent of the weir. There is a grey wagtail about, and sand martins, swallows and swifts are flying at their various feeding heights above the water.

On another stretch of river, we are standing on a bridge when a kingfisher flies underneath. It zooms up on the other side, climbs into the air and hovers over the water before it sees us and is off in a flash. There are more displaying common sandpipers, and territory bargaining is going on among the dippers. Three are on a single rock, and one is displaying to the other two. Later, I find a juvenile dipper, which is very grey and sombre next to the crisp colouring of its parents. It is begging for food, and the adult, out in the river, submerges several times to catch morsels for its offspring.

Besthorpe, 14th May

A typically windy spring day. Swifts, swallows, sand martins and house martins are working ceaselessly, keeping low because their

Adult and juvenile dippers.
Shropshire. May.

Redwings. Highland region. June.

insect prey is being swept under the banks by the wind. A few turtle doves have arrived – really immaculate birds. The only other bird of note in a very uneventful afternoon is a single little ringed plover.

SCOTLAND

Highland region, 31st May

Our first stop on a fine, calm evening is beside a shallow loch where we can hear snipe and redshanks. A pair of greenshanks climb into the evening sky and disappear under the sun, spiralling and calling. On the shore are stonechats, wheatears, meadow pipits and pied wagtails. Among the scattering of ducks on the water – wigeons, tufted ducks and mallards – a pair of pintails stands out. The duck is feeding continuously, with the drake just keeping watch and escorting her. After about an hour, the pintails take off and fly the length of the

Great black-back gull and mallards.
Highland region. June.

loch to disappear at the west end into the rushes which probably hold their nest. On our way round the shore of the loch, we flush another duck pintail from a likely nesting patch of rushes, which is as yet without a nest.

Highland region, 1st June

We move out early from our camp site to inspect the head of another loch. The water is mirror-calm. Two black-throated divers are gliding along close to the shore and, way out in the centre, crossing the loch, are seven mallard ducklings with their mother. In attendance is a great black-back gull, and it is easy to see what he fancies for breakfast. He makes a half-hearted dive at the brood. They all dive, leaving the adult to fend him off. He loses interest and moves away. The ducklings may well be a bit too big for him. The sound of a redwing singing attracts us to an area of gorse and alders where we find two nests with parents feeding their young and one well fledged brood out of the nest. Other species here are siskin, greylag goose and merganser.

Travelling on, we reach a high moorland loch, an altogether bleaker setting. It is overcast and quiet, almost oppressive at times, with not many birds – just some dunlins and golden plovers calling from the peat hags, and some wigeons on the loch. We find a wood sandpiper lurking quietly in a reedy bay. A young golden eagle flies right across the skyline and over the loch; his white wing flashes show well against the dark backdrop of the mountains.

Pintail and golden eagle. Highland region. June.

Hooded crow, curlew, ring ouzels, mistle thrush, buzzard. Highland region. June.

95

Highland region, 2nd June

Dunlin. Highland region. June.

As we drive south along the side of a great loch, everything is quiet until we catch sight of some aerial activity on a bluff by the road. A buzzard is sitting on a birch stump being mobbed by a pair of ring ouzels, a mistle thrush, a curlew and a hooded crow – quite a little drama, in which the poor buzzard looks uncomfortable at having brought together such a disparate group when there is so much space for them all to be in. The reason for the ring ouzels' excitement is that they have their young – two dark slate-grey creatures with darker barring on the flanks and upper parts – out of the nest on the bluff.

On the first loch I come to today are a pair of mergansers and a pair of wigeons, with common gulls sitting in groups on the water. Walking along a bank of heather, we flush a wigeon from its nest, which contains eight creamy white eggs. The nests of the common gulls are hidden on a rocky islet, some scattered along its crown, others by rocks, under old branches or in deep herbage. Just as we are leaving, the black-throated divers appear quite close. One of them, probably the female, has just come off the nest and does a belly-roll to preen. She disappears quite quickly, probably back to the island.

Back on the high moorland, we cross some particularly damp ground and flush a dunlin from four eggs in a nest that looks like a miniature of a snipes' nest surrounded by sphagnum moss. Later in the day, we hear a golden plover and a bird flies from a nest with three eggs almost at our feet. The camouflage plumage of the wings and back makes it very difficult to see among the similarly coloured grasses and mosses. Usually, golden plovers leave the nest when you are still at quite a distance.

Slavonian grebe and little grebes. Highland region. June.

96

Highland region, 3rd June

We get up at four to take an early morning look at the high moorland loch. Apart from the dunlin singing, it is very quiet, as many of the birds are sitting on eggs. To my astonishment, in a reedy corner of the loch that we have passed several times in the last few days, there is a Slavonian grebe looking absolutely magnificent – golden tufts, red eyes and orange plumage. Close by is a pair of little grebes with three young. Now my attention is attracted by some flecks of white water out on the loch. One black-throated diver is in close pursuit of another, with a third standing off from them – possibly two males and a female. They career round the loch at high speed with heads thrust forward, bodies and wings out of the water, half running, half flying as they tear around. It is possible that a rival male has come to the loch and is being shown that the territory is already well occupied. At half past seven, I hear a brief snatch of wood sandpiper song in the distance, but then the bitter cold becomes too much for me and I retire for breakfast. As we near the car, a common sandpiper flutters off four eggs in a typical nesting site on a roadside bank.

Highland region, 4th June

When we emerge from the tent on a damp morning, there are two twites feeding at the edge of the camping area. Both have yellow bills when they are supposed to have grey ones at this time of year – perhaps no-one has told them. After lunch, the rain eases enough for us to return to the moorland loch. On a small rushy pool are a party of seven young teal and another that has somehow ended up at the other

Young snipes. Highland region. June.

Common gulls and a common sandpiper.
Highland region. June.

Teal ducklings, greenshank, common
sandpipers, red-throated diver, fulmar.
Highland region. June.

end of the water. These tiny black and cream buttons of fluff speed
along the water and huddle together under a heather bank when they
seem to be cornered by us; their parents give frantic displays in the
background. As we have found the corpses of two teal ducklings in
the last two days, their mortality rate must be quite high.

We have now arrived at another favourite locale, where we hope to
see an osprey. We settle down to cook our bacon and eggs in the sunshine, but the osprey fails to appear. It is only when we have cleared
up and are ready to move on that we see one way out over the loch. It
is circling, patrolling, hovering and having to put up with a bit of har-
rassment from a great black-back gull. We drive off down a small road
that takes us quite close to it just as it has set its sights on some prey.
It closes its wings to drop down, feet hanging all the while, checks
momentarily to get its stoop just right, then closes its wings again and
goes straight down into the water. Its head and wings emerge from
the great splash with a bit of flapping as it hauls itself up into the air
with a great fish in its talons. It gradually gains height until it has
achieved sufficient altitude and then drifts away, doubtless to its nest.

The sea loch is full of birds. The males among the many eiders are
crooning constantly. On a grassy area with large stony patches is a
ternery inhabited mainly by common terns but with a few pairs of
Arctic terns. There are two oystercatcher nests, one with three eggs
and one with young. On the edge of a grassy field, we find four eider
nests, two of which are built on a basis of dried seaweed from the
high-tide line.

Fulmars are wheeling around the high cliffs just inland from here
and more of them inhabit a ruin out on the edge of the loch. Noises
are coming from some nearby trees, and I find a fulmar sitting on an
old rook's nest; a little later, another comes and perches near it. At the
rate they are spreading, fulmars seem set fair to take over the world.

On a more remote beach at the seaward end of the loch there are a
pair of little terns and one of ringed plovers. Here, too, there are a
few common and Arctic terns and a throng of gulls feeding near the
water's edge.

Later in the day, on some marsh, I find two baby snipe, which are
cheeping anxiously, having been left by a parent that is nowhere to be
seen. From the marshy bay, the calls of a pair of greenshanks, which
must certainly have young, echo along the hillside. In the early evening,
a wood sandpiper starts to sing, rising high into the blue sky. As we
are watching it, a peregrine falcon passes through.

Late in the evening, as we follow the course of a river away from
the loch, we see a trail of bubbles leaving the bank and describing a
semicircle in the black water. The trail of bubbles returns to the bank
just beneath us, where an otter surfaces. It stares straight at us for

what seems like a few seconds, then submerges again leaving another little trail of bubbles. It is only the second otter I have seen, and we have been close enough to make out its whiskers.

Black-necked grebes.
Highland region. June.

Highland region, 7th June

On our last day in the Highlands, we make a few more loch-side stops. One gives a view from the road of a red-throated diver and another provides the sight of black-necked grebes, which are a little more subtle in their plumage than Slavonian grebes but nevertheless splendid birds. Three young are being fed by one pair, while another pair is accompanied by a larger bird, which seems quite old and appears to be assuming the winter plumage pattern. Other sightings today are crested tits with young, a family of Scottish crossbills and a capercaillie with recently hatched young hidden in the undergrowth. The magnificent hen bird creeps around us in the herbage with its great turtle-like head peering at us out of the grass.

100

Black tern. Besthorpe. June.

Fulmars and shags. Highland region.
June.

ENGLAND

Besthorpe, 11th June

Back on home ground on a warm, overcast day, the first bird I see is a handsome summer plumage black tern; it has a black head, sooty underparts and wings that glisten silver in the dull light. It is perched on one of the posts in the water where the black-headed gulls assemble near their nests. Indeed, they are occupying most of the other posts now, apart from one with a common tern on it. Two redshanks are busily proclaiming that they have young, and a green sandpiper, probably a non-breeding bird, takes wing and flies south. It is once again the time of the year when the lapwings start to gather, and the ducks are also on the increase, with twenty tufted ducks and fifty mallards here at the moment. The swans have another brood of three tiny cygnets, which swim across the pool behind their parents. A pair of Canada geese has three goslings, and there is one well-grown stripey-headed young great crested grebe with a parent. Turtle doves go busily to and fro between their nesting areas and the rivulets where they drink out on the gravel workings.

SCOTLAND

Highland region, 24th June

A quick trip north to look at a sea-bird cliff. As you get out to the cliff, you are greeted by a wall, not just of sound, but also of smell. Countless birds are wheeling and diving, calling, crying, shouting, screaming, with the voices of the kittiwakes predominating in the clamour. The water is covered in auks – razorbills, guillemots and a few puffins – and there are fulmars everywhere. As you peer over the edge of the cliff, nesting fulmars gaze nervously at you and are liable at any moment to spit their foul yellow vomit at you; sometimes they leave the nest to reveal a single white egg.

The white-splashed cliffs are crowned with short grass and pink-flowered clumps of thrift. Up here, the jackdaws breed; their tatty, spiky-headed young look at you with wild eyes, unsure whether to stay or flee. They flop off to another part of the cliff top. A dark phase Arctic skua, sleek and suitably piratical in appearance, works the cliff top and then drifts out to sea and makes a sudden lunge at a kitti-wake. Rock doves zoom in and out of caves.

The activity on these cliffs is incessant. Ledges of guillemots are all shaking their heads from side to side, their eyes searching. Guillemots have the nasty habit of defecating on their neighbours; their constant visits to the sea may have functions apart from food gathering. The razorbills tend to pick less public nesting places than the guillemots, secreting themselves in little holes and crevices. The young of both species wander around perilously among the adults on the ledges. The guillemots include birds of the bridled form, with white spectacles on the usual chocolate colour of the head. The colony does not in-clude many puffins, and one of the slopes with their burrows seems to have been invaded by fulmars, although there are still about a dozen puffins standing at one edge of it.

Kittiwakes seem beautifully docile creatures; tired from feeding their young, many of them are asleep on the nest. The young move their heads as one piece of activity after another catches their eye. The kittiwakes periodically have dreads – sudden flights. A whole stream of them will emerge noisily from a cliff face or a cave and surge out to sea where they disperse and drift quietly back to the cliff.

Kittiwakes. Highland region. June.

The shags like to nest in cool shadowy spots in deep clefts near the bases of the cliffs. The young are like toy replicas of their parents, covered in grey down. The adults move their necks and bodies sinuously as they keep watch and glisten dark green, then black, then white as the light catches their bodies. On the sea, five eiders – three female and two immature – look up at the show on the cliff above them. On one of the weed-covered slabs of rock in the sea, a bonxie – great skua – is tearing at the flesh of an auk that it must recently have killed. The five eiders continue on their way past this macabre scene.

Highland region, 25th June

Early morning on a coastal moorland – we wake to the cries of red-throated divers. Out on the moorland, we soon come to Arctic skua territory. One bird with a brown body and pale creamy face has a nest with one egg; it is joined by its mate, which is a dark phase bird. A bonxie appears and is chivvied by the Arctic skuas. It attracts a hooded crow and brings it to the ground. A pair of peregrine falcons come over *en route* from a hunting mission – they will have large young by now. The two Arctic skuas fly up to inspect the peregrines and start a mild dogfight in the air before realising the implications and returning to ground. There is a garrulous group of six red-throated divers on one of the lochs. Three of them break away and race across the water with their necks straight out like sticks.

We see another pair of Arctic skuas, just like the last ones: one light, one dark, and a nest with one egg. Parties of two or three great skuas are flying ominously around the moorland. One pair of these bonxies is definitely on its nesting territory, and, as we approach the nest, we are spectacularly dive-bombed: birds zoom in, braking with tail and feet six feet from our heads and passing with a great whoosh of wings. Another pair comes to help them in repelling the invaders.

ENGLAND

Besthorpe, 2nd July

The heron families are now coming into the marsh, driving the black-headed gulls frantic and pursuing them vigorously until they leave for somewhere quieter. A group of nine is far out on an arable field and looks very disgruntled. Turtle doves, wood pigeons and stock doves are all coming in to feed and drink.

Besthorpe, 15th July

On a steamy, hot evening, a party of mistle thrushes is sitting in a field as I approach the gravel workings, from which come the ominous sounds of machinery. Now that the gravel has been worked out, the whole area is being given back to agriculture. In other words, one of the finest bird places in Nottinghamshire is being destroyed for a few more superfluous acres of wheat.

Arctic skuas. Highland region. June.

Reddish egrets, roseate spoonbills,
white ibises and wood storks. Sanibel
Island, Florida. September.

Blakeney Point, Norfolk, 28th July

Turtle doves. Besthorpe. July.

Our early morning walk coincides with high tide, and there are plenty of resting and roosting waders close enough for good visibility. A flock of about twenty summer plumage knots flies over the shingle, and we also find about twenty little terns, a good number to see in one place. There are a few young kittiwakes around.

Because there is a strong on-shore breeze, we walk on the estuary side of the point, where there are greenshanks, many redshanks and a few whimbrels, but then we find a party of about 120 roosting whimbrels with a curlew, one or two bar-tailed godwits, turnstones and an oystercatcher.

It is pleasing to see so many terns nesting at the end of the point. In fact, the whole area of Blakeney and Cley is as good as it was when I started visiting it twenty-five years ago. Particularly notable today is a large secondary colony of Sandwich terns which apparently came late in the nesting season and is now established on one of the far spits. Many of the terns have young that are only a few days old.

Arctic skua and Sandwich tern.
Anderby, August.

As the tide drops, it uncovers the sandbars, on which the birds land to rest – some of the terns from the shingle and small parties of waders, including some sanderlings in summer plumage. A group of kittwakes looks very dispirited when I remember how active and fulfilled they seemed on the sea cliffs in the Highlands.

On Cley marshes, the number of waders is quite surprising for the end of July: spotted redshanks, including one bird that is still quite dark, lots of ruffs, with the moulting males in blotchy, rather comical plumage, two adult little stints, several handsome adult curlew sandpipers, many showing the red underparts of their summer dress, and a fine party of black-tailed godwits.

Besthorpe, 21st August

A great crested grebe almost in winter plumage glints in the summer sunlight. Juvenile common terns pestering their parents for food intrude noisily on the late August torpor. The wreckers' machinery lies quiet, observing the Sabbath. On each horizon, smoke drifts gently skyward from the stubble-burning, as if from a distant battlefield. A juvenile heron stands, considering whether or not to stay. Small numbers of teal rest, sleep or preen. On a lagoon that is being filled in with fly ash, twenty-one great crested grebes are sleeping, surrounded by a large number of mallards and several great black-back gulls. A sedge warbler, soon to depart for a better place, calls from a bank.

Anderby, 28th August

A brisk north-easterly wind is coming in off quite a rough sea. An Arctic skua pursues a Sandwich tern as other terns and gulls pass by. Far out, young gannets and Arctic skuas shear down wind, imitating shearwaters in their movement. A search of the sycamores and buckthorns does not reveal any migrant small birds but only the resident goldfinches, blue tits and robins. The ringed plovers have managed to nest and raise their young here in spite of the disturbance from people and particularly dogs, which are a real menace on beaches. The adult ringed plovers have had to protect their young by leading the dogs an endless dance down to the mud at the water's edge and back again. Their success in breeding against such odds is very encouraging.

Gibraltar Point, 7th September

An afternoon twitch for a citrine wagtail. We quickly locate it – an immature bird, which is very grey and presents many identification problems, but seems to be the real thing. It gives its diagnostic call several times as it flies, and we get one close-up view of it right below the hide.

Curlew, whimbrel, oystercatcher, curlew sandpipers, ruffs, little stints. North Norfolk. July.

Citrine wagtail. Gibraltar Point, Lincolnshire. September.

Pileated woodpecker. Corkscrew
Swamp, Florida. September.

UNITED STATES: Autumn

Above:
Anhingas. Sanibel Island, Florida.
September.
Right:
Carolina wren. Corkscrew Swamp,
Florida. September.

Tamiami Trail, Florida, 16th September

The Tamiami trail is a straight highway that cuts westwards across the northern part of the Everglades. Parallel to the road on both sides are almost continuous water channels, and beyond these stretches a virtually undeveloped wilderness of swamp and woodland. There are so many birds to be seen that looking and driving at the same time becomes something of a hazard. The journey produces a particularly good range of herons – great blue, little blue, green, and Louisiana herons, great, snowy and cattle egrets – as well as white ibises and one or two waders. The greatest excitement, though, is the snail kite, a basically South American species that has its only regular breeding place on the North American mainland here in Florida. The two we see are female or immature, and not very spectacular, but we are able to see the curved bill that is the particular adaptation of this species to allow it to feed on snails, its main food. Another sight that becomes increasingly frequent as we drive is of belted kingfishers perched on roadside wires, high above the waterways, looking down for prey. Before reaching Corkscrew Swamp, we spot at least thirty of these birds, many more than I have seen on previous trips. Turkey vultures and black vultures are circling high up but some are feeding on the road. It is frustrating to drive the Tamiami Trail, which is a fast, smooth highway, much of it with nowhere to pull off and park, so that there is no alternative but to drive past birds you have sighted and hope to get an identification through the car window. However, we manage to see another rare bird of the area, a smooth-billed ani, from the roadside.

Clouds have been building up all morning and form a fitting background for the anhingas that patrol over the marsh woodlands like sinister, angular spy-planes. As we arrive at Corkscrew Swamp, hoping

Limpkin. Corkscrew Swamp, Florida.
September.

to get two or three hours' walking in the cypress swamps, the whole sky blackens and the thunderstorm breaks. Wind and rain lash the palm trees and bring back vivid memories of hurricane scenes in old movies, although the storm is nowhere near hurricane force.

Corkscrew Swamp, Florida, 17th September

The swamp is an unforgettable place, with great bald cypress trees hundreds of years old and great roots forming a tracery around the trunks. There are clouds of Spanish moss in the foliage, and bromeliads grow on branches that descend into the black water and continue in reflection. It is intensely humid, like being wrapped in hot, wet blankets. The National Audubon Society deserves the highest praise for saving this undisturbed remnant of the original country, and for preserving and managing it so efficiently.

It is perhaps not the most productive time of year to come here, but there is still plenty to see. Anhingas patrol the sky on endless missions and vultures, mainly turkey vultures, float about overhead. One of the best sights on this visit is the pileated woodpecker, a huge, handsome bird, which I see twice at very close range as it hammers at the trees. There are quite a lot of Carolina wrens, but otherwise the score of small birds is not very high: two prothonotary warblers, a blue-gray gnatcatcher, several white-eyed vireos and a thrush, probably a gray-cheeked thrush, which I could not keep in sight for long enough to identify. Raptors are represented by some very noisy red-shouldered hawks. There are baby alligators and lots of different coloured butterflies – I wish I knew more about them.

My prime target here is the limpkin, which holds out until I am within a quarter of an hour of leaving before emerging from the thick vegetation on the edge of one of the lettuce swamps. It is feeding in a very deliberate way, probing, striding and picking between the vegetation, and delicately fetching out a snail. After a while, it is disturbed and flies over to another patch with thick grass and vanishes – there could be fifty more of them in that patch without anyone knowing.

Sanibel Island, Florida, 18th September

We start with a morning drive through the 'Ding' Darling National Wildlife Refuge, a large area of mangroves on the east of the island, which has the drive-through facilities that you come to expect in the National Parks. One of the first birds we see is a magnificent frigatebird – a first for me – soaring high above the mangroves. Herons are everywhere, and, among the little blue herons, we see a reddish egret, which makes strange jerking, dancing movements as its probes and feeds in the water. Also wading around among the mangroves are roseate spoonbills, white ibises, green herons, various egrets and an immature little blue heron, which, surprisingly, is all white and might be mistaken for one of the white egrets except for its blue bill.

There are numerous pied-billed grebes, the first I have seen in North America in five trips. My only previous record of this species was way back in 1965 on the Chew Valley Reservoir in Somerset. Flying above the mangroves are more magnificent frigatebirds and everywhere there are anhingas, which seem to be very common. An osprey glides overhead, and turkey vultures circle. Brown pelicans drift lazily over the lagoons.

We drive to one of the beaches at the north end of the island. Sanibel is famous for shells, and small specimens cover the beach. Although it is high tide and there are a good few people around, the resting shore birds seem able to share the amenities with humans. Big parties of willets have sanderlings, turnstones and black-bellied plovers among

Snail kite, red-shouldered hawk, prothonotary warbler. Florida. September.

Louisiana herons. Sanibel Island, Florida. September.

Anhingas. Sanibel Island,
Florida. September.

them, and there are Sandwich terns and laughing gulls, all in scattered groups just a bit up from the water, where people are walking.

A lunchtime return to the 'Ding' Darling Reserve produces most of the species that we saw earlier, although the middle of the day has lessened the amount of bird activity. The trip is made worthwhile by turkey vulture that allows us to park right by it as it devours a fish carcase on the verge.

In the afternoon, on the beaches by the lighthouse, small groups of birds congregate: again, Sandwich terns, laughing gulls, sanderlings,

Turkey vulture. Sanibel Island, Florida. September.

and a few black-bellied plovers and willets. Brown pelicans are flying around but focusing their attention on what turns out to be a pier built out into the water for fishing. There are pelicans perching on a roof section and swimming around underneath the pier, hoping for titbits.

Back again in the 'Ding' Darling Reserve in the early evening, just before dusk, the tide is dropping, uncovering large areas of mud among the mangroves. The number of herons is now really remarkable, with yellow-crowned and black-crowned night herons and a few reddish egrets among the more common species. A green heron lands high in a dead mangrove and is still flapping about, trying to get a footing, when a dragonfly comes past and the bird's neck shoots out in a vain attempt to capture it.

Sanibel Island, 19th September

The first patch of water I find on an early morning visit to the 'Ding' Darling Reserve has some mud and a good collection of birds: wood storks, the first on this trip, three or four roseate spoonbills, white ibis, greater yellowlegs, reddish egret and sundry other herons, all seen against the black water and backlit by the rising sun. I am tempted to put the telescope up and do some sketching, but I am immediately driven back into the car by the insects. It is not even possible to have a window open without suffering, and the only solution is to sit with the air-conditioning on.

After a mid-day thunderstorm and a visit to the fishing pier where the pelicans share the roof space with other fish-eaters – snowy egret, little blue heron and fish crow – I return in the evening to the 'Ding' Darling Reserve. Large areas of mud are now exposed, and there are plenty of birds, including small waders, which could be western sandpipers, but the light is not good enough for a firm identification. As dusk comes, a raccoon appears across the water, working his way through the lower storey of mangroves and occasionally making forays out to the water's edge. The reddish egret and the snowy egret stir the mud with their feet and then look to see what small prey has been disturbed. Anhingas hang in the trees like enormous prehistoric bats. One of the islands in a nearby bay is a roost for the egrets which are pouring in. It is encrusted in white dots and stands out like a Christmas cake against the darkening green of the vegetation.

Sanibel Island, 20th September

Today it is not as good at the 'Ding' Darling reserve as it was yesterday morning – perhaps I have come too early; what little mud there is lies between me and the sun. However, there is by far the largest

Little blue heron. Sanibel Island, Florida. September.

number yet of reddish egrets – I can count about thirty in one lagoon. I venture along a track, providing a feast for the mosquitoes, and see an ovenbird, a prairie warbler and a yellow warbler. There are a few blue-winged teal about, and overhead are frigatebirds and one or two ospreys. I have a close view of a little blue heron stalking over some mangrove roots and, behind him, dead mangroves full of anhingas sitting just drying and waiting.

I return from the morning visit and decide to cool off by taking a swim. There is a lot to be said for a swimming pool from which you can watch frigatebirds and ospreys overhead and hear the chorus of fish crows from a nearby roof.

Magnificent frigatebirds. Sanibel Island, Florida. September.

Sanibel Island and Fort Myers, Florida, 21st September

Today's early morning visit is to a tract of small ponds, scrub and bushy rides, where the insect level is decidedly English, a pleasant change from the mangrove swamps. The most obvious signs of the autumn migration are the small groups of up to a dozen eastern king-birds in the tree-tops, mainly on bare branches, from which they are flycatching. Other birds here are prairie warblers, blue-gray gnat-catchers, brown thrashers, rufous-sided towhees and, a Florida special, smooth-billed anis. These are rather grotesque black members of the cuckoo family with over-large stubby bills.

Towards the end of the morning, we arrive at Fort Myers beach. At the edge of the sand is a row of giant monoliths, one of which is the Holiday Inn, where we park. Immediately off the beach, a spit of sand runs parallel to the shore enclosing a narrow creek which is noted for shorebirds. I first look at a group of at least two hundred dowitchers, which seem to be short-billed rather than the very similar long-billed species. In addition, there are a long-billed curlew, two marbled godwits, one Wilson's phalarope and a few whimbrels as well as sundry willets and black-bellied plovers and a ring-billed gull. I find some shade from one of the buildings where I can stand to watch the birds through the telescope and sketch them, but then I move out into the full heat of the spit itself. Even the waders are all lying down. Here there are semipalmated plovers and some Wilson's plovers, both species of ringed plover: the Wilson's, a chunky bird with a hefty bill, is a scarce inhabitant of eastern and southern beaches. There are lots of small waders, too: dunlins and peeps – probably least and western sandpipers, but I shall come back for a more careful look when it is cooler. American birds seem much more ready than British ones to share the beach with humans: the roosting waders are quite close to the sunbathers.

Smooth-billed ani. Sanibel Island, Florida. September.

Sanibel Island and Fort Myers, 22nd September

Early morning on the beach. The rising sun makes the white sand glow pinkish orange. With low tide uncovering the sandbar, a host of Sandwich terns and laughing gulls have gathered. There are also one or two snowy egrets and a royal tern, a splendid specimen with a huge orange bill, shaggy black crest and white forehead. A lone frigatebird is flying high, and there are pelicans moving down towards the fishing pier. Even out at the edge of the water, the insects are still biting.

Just after midday, I return to the heat of Fort Myers beach and confirm that the peeps are mostly western sandpipers with just a few least sandpipers among them. These small sandpipers are extremely similar and when odd individual peeps turn up in Britain, they can cause great identification problems. The best way to sort them out seems to be to concentrate on the size, shape and structure, rather than the plumage, of the bird. There are at least forty Wilson's plovers, which is quite a good party of this species; many of them seem to be juveniles. In addition, there are a lot of snowy plovers, tiny birds of a washed-out colour that are very inconspicuous on the sand. The wader flock is perhaps slightly smaller than it was yesterday. The marbled godwits have gone but the Wilson's phalarope is still here and there are a few knots (or red knots as they are called on this side of the Atlantic) among the dowitchers.

After nearly a week of walking the beaches of the Gulf coast, I have realised that something is missing: there is virtually no man-made debris – no lumps of expanded polystyrene, no plastic mugs or bottles, no glass jars, no beer cans. All that turns up is the natural beach debris of seaweed and so on, which seems amazing when we are so close to well-populated areas.

Blue-gray gnatcatcher, ovenbird, yellow-throated warbler. Sanibel Island, Florida. September.

Sanibel Island and Fort Myers, 23rd September

Another early morning walk around the lighthouse area to look for migrants. There is a fresh south-easterly breeze, and lots of birds are on the move. Three ospreys, probably residents, are playing around the lighthouse. Kingbirds, which, as far as I can make out, are all eastern kingbirds, fly over in small groups of up to twenty at a time, all heading roughly south. Large numbers of warblers are also on the wing, but mainly so high up that they are impossible to identify. Although some are calling, I am not familiar enough with their calls to be able to make identifications from them. A few birds do land in the trees to feed: a small party of prairie warblers, an immature male American redstart, a yellow-throated warbler, a probable Blackburnian warbler and an immature palm warbler. The usual shore birds and the blue-gray gnatcatchers, ovenbirds and brown thrasher from yesterday are still here and there are several cardinals, which are probably residents. A noisy gathering of fish crows on the beach decides what to do for the morning and departs.

At lunchtime, I return to Fort Myers beach to sort out a few questions about the waders. I identified snowy plovers yesterday, but did not go through the similar birds thoroughly enough to see if there were any piping plovers among them. I can now see that there are piping plovers in winter plumage with black, stubby bills and ochre legs and snowy plovers with slightly longer black bills and dark grey legs. The piping plovers are also slightly browner in their upper parts. Another reason for coming back here is to have yet another look at the dowitchers, which are, on the whole, I think, short-billed rather than long-billed. One or two are still virtually in summer plumage with spotted rather than barred flanks, and the winter plumage birds almost all have spotted under-tail coverts, a good clue to their identity. Their low, conversational tyu-tyu sounds are characteristic of the short-billed species. Today's new arrivals are an immature royal tern and several Forster's terns, which are about the size of common terns but have pale wingtips and a distinctive black mask and ear-patches.

Immature royal tern and Forster's tern. Fort Myers, Florida. September.

Sanibel Island, 24th September

My last early morning visit to the lighthouse area. The first bird of note is a female merlin, which slips in over the trees and then departs, but soon another or perhaps the same merlin appears, making an unsuccessful bid to put starling on the breakfast menu. There is still much migration in progress. Several rough-winged swallows and one or two kingbirds fly overhead, but the most evident movement this morning is of warblers, which come through in parties – fives, tens and twenties – calling as they go, some high, some just catching the treetops and pausing for a moment before continuing on their way south; a few come in to land. There are some more American red-starts including one superb male, and today's new species are the black-and-white warbler and the northern parula. A royal tern cuts the corner across the lighthouse area calling shrilly, followed by a horde of Sandwich terns. There are ospreys and a turkey vulture around, and the pelicans are going towards the fishing pier for their day's work. By far the most impressive sight, though, is the spectacle of the countless tiny warblers high against the early morning greyness, glinting in the rising sun as they head south across the Gulf of Mexico.

Merritt Island, Florida, 25th September

At dusk, a look around the Merritt Island National Wildlife Refuge, which lies in the area of Cape Canaveral and the John F. Kennedy Space Center, produces a party of over thirty roseate spoonbills. Forty black skimmers are gathered, possibly in a roost, on one of the muddy pools. There is a stiff onshore breeze, and, by the NASA causeway, we see a parasitic jaeger, which is the splendid American name for the Arctic skua.

Merritt Island, 26th September

A particularly fine sight among a host of birds early this morning is the roost of black skimmers that we found yesterday evening. With all the birds on the ground, I count over a hundred, many of which are immature. With them are seven Caspian terns, and nearby is a small group of Forster's terns; there are also a few wood storks. Later, we come upon a great assemblage of herons, ibises and spoonbills on what is obviously a very rich feeding patch. Perhaps 150 birds in all are moving with the feed. In the middle are snowy and great egrets with a few roseate spoonbills among them and a large group of white ibises nearby; around the edge are Louisiana herons, with one or two reddish egrets doing their usual dance on the periphery. The waders here are killdeers, semipalmated and black-bellied plovers, lesser yellowlegs and a lot of peeps, mainly in the distance – the few that come close enough for me to make an attempt at identifying them seem mainly to be semipalmated sandpipers. The ducks, and there are a lot of them, are invariably between me and the early morning sun, which reduces them to silhouettes; certainly they include a great number of blue-winged teal and a few northern shovelers.

Belted kingfisher. Merritt Island, Florida. September.

As we tour the John F. Kennedy Space Center and the NASA and US Air Force aerospace complex, which cover a vast area of Merritt Island and Cape Canaveral, I am pleased to see how the acquisition of this land by the government many years ago has saved thousands of acres of coastline from being ruined by holiday development. A belted kingfisher is perched on a sign right in front of the huge gantry from which the space shuttle *Challenger* is launched, and, on the grassland in front of the vehicle assembly building, many cattle egrets are gathered.

Later, at Playalinda beach, on the fringe of the NASA area, we

American redstart with ospreys.
Sanibel. September.

Overleaf:
Royal tern with laughing gulls, Sandwich
terns and snowy egret. Sanibel Island,
Florida. September.

watch a couple of ospreys, which are perched on dead trees in one of
the lagoons. While we are watching the ospreys, a female peregrine
falcon flashes over the lagoon, momentarily dislodging one of the
ospreys from its perch. It flaps in an ungainly way for a few moments;
by the time it has regained its composure and settled down again, the
peregrine has gone. On the road, a group of turkey vultures is feeding
off a freshly killed armadillo. The stiff onshore breeze gives the beach
itself a coolness that reminds me of the Lincolnshire coast. There are
sanderlings and terns down by the sea, and more terns are feeding out
at sea, among them three royal terns and a Forster's tern, and laughing
gulls and one or two brown pelicans pass along the coast. Coming
back along the Max Hoeck trail, we find a couple of glossy ibises, the
first I have seen on this trip.

In the evening, we drive along the Black Point Road through the
reserve. Before we reach the start of the road, we see an adult bald

119

eagle perched in a dead tree, a very typical place for one to be. There are so many ospreys around that you have to be careful not to overlook an eagle as just another osprey. This evening, there are more glossy ibises – two parties, one feeding in the lagoon and the other flying over the reserve.

Bald eagle. Merritt Island, Florida. September.

Rocky Neck State Park, Connecticut, 30th September

This is not such a good place for birds in the autumn as in the spring, and there are not as many birds as when we came here last year. Out on the marsh, there are still a few snowy egrets, a great blue heron and a small party of black ducks. The waders are a couple of killdeers, a small group of greater yellowlegs and two least sandpipers. The osprey nest is there with a warning to people not to disturb it, but the ospreys appear to have left the area for the time being.

Montauk Point and Moriches Bay, Long Island, New York, 4th October

Just after dawn, and the sun is a red ball rising from a misty sea. There are high, twittering groups of birds on the move. Thrushes dive out of the sky down into the bushes and vanish before I can get a good view. The foghorn drones relentlessly, and the greatest bird activity is a huge mass of gulls and terns, several hundred birds, which must have found a shoal of fish. There are many herring gulls, a few great blackbacks and one or two smaller gulls. The terns appear to be mainly common and Arctic, but I spot a Forster's tern, which comes a bit closer than the rest. A fine pale phase parasitic jaeger appears but seems daunted by the sheer number of terns and drifts away without making much effort.

On the way from Montauk Point to Moriches Bay, which is on the south side of Long Island, we see a red-tailed hawk, two sharp-shinned hawks and numerous flickers. We drive the length of the great barrier beach that runs down towards Fire Island. What a dismal sight it is: this once magnificent beach is totally built up with a grotesque ghost town of shacks and shanties, some no doubt very elaborate and expensive, but the whole a grisly reminder of what can happen to a beautiful area of seashore in the absence of planning restrictions.

At Cupsogue, we come within the area of National Seashore and there is no building, just the long beach running between the open sea and the great expanse of Moriches Bay on the inside. The high tide is just turning, and there are hosts of gulls, terns and egrets some distance away. As I walk out into the area of dunes, a party of horned larks on the sand runs off through the golden rod and then flies away.

Greater yellowlegs. Rocky Neck State Park, Connecticut. September.

In the late afternoon, we return to Montauk Point, again in search of migrants. Within a short time, I see a yellowthroat, a thrush, which I cannot immediately name and a warbler that could well be a Connecticut warbler – two things to check later. The biggest excitement of the evening is a party of ten cedar waxwings, whose shrill cries attract our attention. They range over a wide area, looking for berries, and return to their favourite vantage point, some high, bare branches overlooking the cliffs near the lighthouse. There are three adults and seven juveniles. As the mist closes in and the foghorn resumes its duty, flights of laughing gulls stream north past the point.

My reference books tell me that this afternoon's thrush was a hermit thrush and the warbler was not a Connecticut but a Nashville warbler.

Montauk Point, 5th October

Here again for another red sunrise. Out at sea, the gulls and terns on their shoals of fish form a boiling silvery mass. A double-crested cormorant sits just offshore, partly submerged, and then takes off to find

Nashville warbler. Montauk Point, Long Island. October.

new fishing places. The laughing gulls which were flighting north last night are now returning south. The local herring and great black-back gulls squabble and fight, watch the fishermen or just laze on the beach. Further along, where some weed has been washed up among the stones, sanderlings, turnstones and semipalmated plovers are feeding in little, scurrying groups. In addition to the Nashville warbler and a single cedar waxwing, there is a fine prairie warbler, which is streaked with black on its bright yellow underparts. The area has a pair of sharp-shinned hawks and another single one.

Jamaica Bay, Long Island, New York, 6th October

Jamaica Bay is familiar territory for me, a pleasure after the work of discovering and exploring new locations. A walk round the west pond shows the typical richness of the bird life here. There are black ducks, American wigeons, mallard, a few blue-winged teal still in eclipse, great blue herons, snowy egrets and a noisy group of Canada geese. Plenty of tree swallows and flickers are moving through, and a pair of sharp-shinned hawks are operating around the garden, as intent as I am on finding small birds. An osprey hangs over the pool and then flies away. With a sudden croak, an American bittern rises from the marsh grass and flies a hundred yards before disappearing again.

The east pond is a much larger stretch of water than the west pond, and beyond it is Kennedy Airport. Many of the aircraft taking off come out over this pool, and I see Concorde for the second time in a couple of hours. The water is covered in ducks until another bird-watcher wades down the side of the pool and flushes most of them. Before he does so, I have noted many American wigeons, some green-winged teal, a few gadwalls and mallard, several northern shovelers and, in the distance, a raft of scaups and some Canada geese. Over the edge of the reeds are two marsh hawks, and a couple of American kestrels fly over the pool. The water level is too high for there to be much mud except out in the centre of the pool, around a collection of sticks and wooden posts. The small group of waders on it is made up of a few dowitchers, a willet, a lesser yellowlegs and one of the birds I have been looking out for on this trip, a stilt sandpiper. It has a very long, slightly decurved bill, greyish upperparts, a strong eye-stripe and a warm grey-brown cap. It wades belly-deep, feeding beside the yellowlegs. Other waders – mainly black-bellied plovers, with a few red knots, sanderlings and dunlins – are flying over the pool, displaced from their feeding spots by the tide.

Stilt sandpiper. Jamaica Bay, Long Island, New York. October.

Double-crested cormorant with laughing
gulls. Montauk Point, Long Island.
October.

BRITAIN: Autumn-Winter

ENGLAND

Spurn Point, Yorkshire, 29th October

It is many years since I was last here, and it is good to be back on a particularly birdy late autumn day. Yesterday evening, there were apparently massive movements of little auks, and, as soon as we start sea-watching, it is evident that they are continuing. Parties of from half a dozen to thirty or forty birds are moving north in steady streams; most are tiny, flickering shapes far out over the sea, but one or two birds are close enough for us to see the details of their plumage. It is a wonder that these diminutive birds survive in the Arctic and throughout the winter gales at sea. Sometimes, of course, they do not survive, as last winter's wreck showed.

After the little auks, the main highlight of the day is seeing a long-eared owl coming in, having obviously flown the North Sea. It flops on the first piece of bank it finds, quite close to about twenty bird-watchers, providing superlative views until another group arrives and presses too close – selfish behaviour that is unfortunately not unusual. The marvellous orange eyes glare, and the bird, obviously exhausted,

Horned larks. Moriches Bay, Long Island. October.

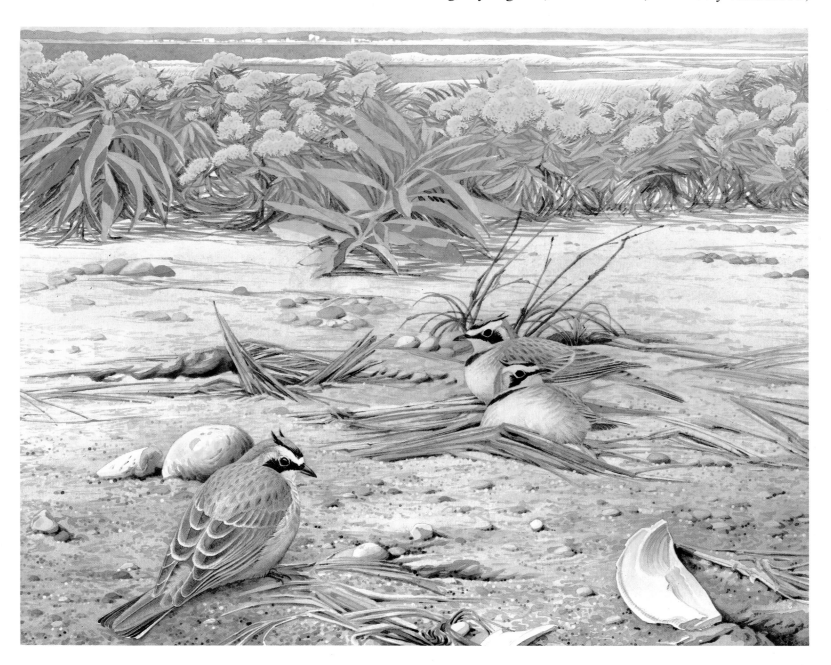

rests for about a quarter of an hour before flying into the bushes by the observatory. This is a bad move, as it then suffers the indignity of being caught and ringed, which is unnecessarily hard on it after such a long journey. Birds of note on the sea are Arctic and great skuas, Manx shearwaters, little gulls, a few divers, goldeneyes and long-tailed ducks. Passerines are also coming in: bramblings, snow buntings and skylarks. A goldcrest flies up the bank, obviously having just come off the water, pauses briefly under the hide and then heads inland.

On the estuary side of Spurn Head, waders are massed along the tide-line: mainly oystercatchers and redshanks, with a few knots, grey plovers, bar-tailed godwits and dunlins. Then, to our amazement, we see about twenty-five little auks bobbing up and down on the water just behind a clump of vegetation and a group of redshanks. After half a minute, they take flight, going along the coast, then over the shore, above the church, and cut back into the estuary without finding the sea. They will probably swim out later.

Long-eared owl. Spurn Point, Yorkshire. October.

Above:
Long-eared owl and little auks. Spurn
Point, Yorkshire. October.
Below:
Redshanks with little auks. Spurn Point,
Yorkshire. October.

Bar-tailed godwits with knots.
Gibraltar Point, Lincolnshire.

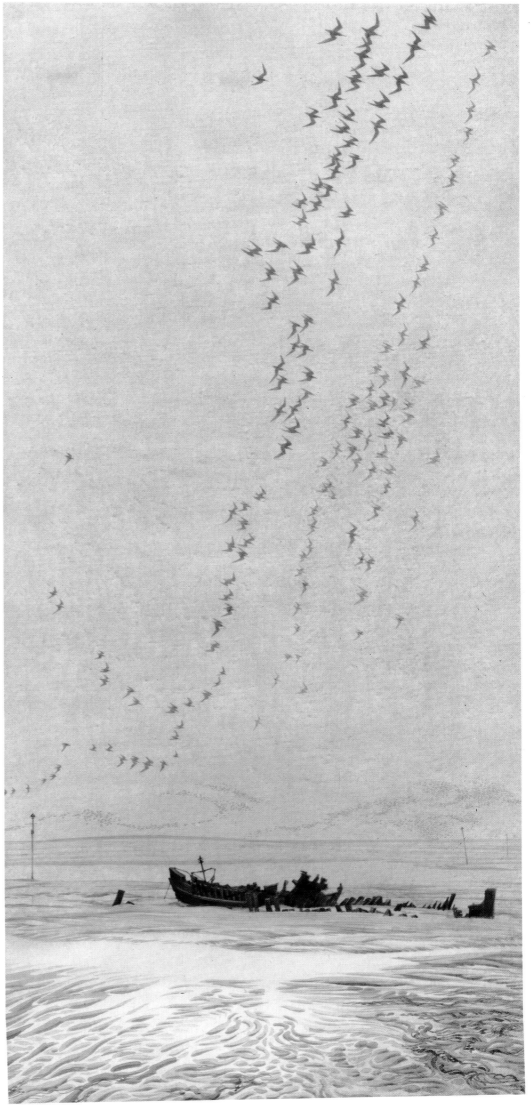